Th.. .. ..

A refreshing approach to a subject that has already been addressed from all perspectives so many times in so many ways. is different – in this book the author presents the ...ics and tools for managing all aspects of a person's activ- oth business and personal. Apply these with care – they ell change your life.

...Ianias FCCA, Chartered Certified Accountant and s Consultant, London, UK

...anks to the author. In 2000 I received my personal ...ased on the material contained in *The Future Is Yours!* to d manage my own company. What I loved about it was licity and how easy it was to apply immediately what I

Zamora, Executive Director, Bogotá, Colombia, South

...

:ry clear and straightforward manner, Rolf U. Kramer ...es the "change of mind" that needs to occur at the core of istrative efficiency, in order to enhance relationships with human beings as well as awaken the sense of responsibility its forms. *The Future Is Yours!* is multi-cultural and :ends all boundaries. I will recommend it to all and sundry, ially to the African mind.

-**Bairo Sabally**, former Vice-President of The Gambia, West a

Why bother with yet another book on managing (and leading) people? The answer is simple. This book is powerfully different and powerfully effective. Most leadership and management books are based on theories and case-study examples. They do not explore and are thus not based on a deep understanding of people, the human spirit and what makes us tick, as individuals and in teams. Rolf U. Kramer's book does exactly that. He provides the reader with a powerful set of generalised principles and explanations organised to be easily understood and built upon. You can rely on them to work in any leadership or management situation in any environment or culture.

David R. J. Powell, MD Corporate Leadership Pty Ltd, Sydney, Australia

Putting the core factors of success in management together whilst keeping an eye on everyday reality is no easy task. Quite often the reader has to stumble over trade jargon or overly abstract examples. Yet Rolf U. Kramer succeeds in highlighting the very components which play their role not only in professional life but also in one's family or the planning of one's personal life. The examples given quite often made me smile; they shed quite a light on the fabric of society.

Markus Novak, Product Manager, Chamber of Commerce, Vienna, Austria

As a mother of twins, part-time assistant to a business coach, MindWalking Trainer, and executive director of a kite-surfing school, I have to meet a multiplicity of challenges. It used to be chaos, and I never knew where to start. But reading *The Future Is Yours!* helped me to separate the various hats I'm wearing and get my priorities straight. Which has done loads for my peace of mind and the harmony of family life. I can recommend this book to anyone, whatever it is they have to manage.

Beate Kürsteiner, multi-tasking housewife, Frankfurt, Germany

The Future Is Yours!

How to effectively manage the whole world, including life, family, and business, and remain true to yourself

The Future Is Yours!

How to effectively manage the
whole world, including life, family,
and business, and remain
true to yourself

Rolf U. Kramer MA

**BUSINESS
BOOKS**

Winchester, UK
Washington, USA

First published by Business Books, 2013
Business Books is an imprint of John Hunt Publishing Ltd., Laurel House, Station Approach,
Alresford, Hants, SO24 9JH, UK
office1@jhpbooks.net
www.johnhuntpublishing.com

For distributor details and how to order please visit the 'Ordering' section on our website.

Text copyright: Rolf U. Kramer 2013

ISBN: 978 1 78279 223 9

A CIP catalogue record for this book is available from the British Library.

Design: Stuart Davies

Printed and bound by CPI Group (UK) Ltd, Croydon, CR0 4YY

We operate a distinctive and ethical publishing philosophy in all
areas of our business, from our global network of authors to
production and worldwide distribution.

CONTENTS

Why This Book?   1

1. Everybody a Manager   3
It all begins with a thought   4
On the nature of a good manager   6
The human condition: being, doing, and having   8
Could work be a game?   11
The team: founders, players, pieces   14
Management: life on a tightrope   15
How bad management can degrade a game   16

2. Creating the Future   19
Concepts and ideals   19
We are powered by dreams   21
How to get things done   24
Levels of action   24
Goals and visions: the difference   25
Spontaneity? – Yes, please!   26
Good rules will keep you out of trouble   26
Only products tell the tale   29
Selling and buying dreams   32
Is it going the right way?   33
How to set up a successful game   35

3. Organisation   39
Putting hats on heads   39
How to build a good team   42
Production and organisation in the right balance   45
Hats and functions   46
An all-purpose Organisational Model   48
The secret is in the hologram   50

Contributions always welcome!   52
Secrecy is an explosive   54
Organisational illnesses   56
The art of delegating work   60

4. Synergetic Leadership   **63**
Seven virtues in communication   63
The logic of emotions   68
Frustration: downward step by step   69
Understanding on three levels   71
The art of motivation   73
What is motivating you?   75
Praise and blame   76
Group decisions made easy   77
The magic of manipulation   82

5. Ethics   **89**
Right and wrong   89
Ethics and morals   92
Three levels of ethics   94
Integrity   96
Integrity levels   99
Production levels   103
Management by ethics   110
Two rights for all game players   111
The value of games   113

Why This Book?

Good management is like walking a tightrope: one risks falling down either one side or the other. Either you are too virtuous to succeed, or you sacrifice all virtue in order to be successful.

A narrow path, indeed!

"The long, steep path towards virtue" is what the Greek poet Hesiod called it a few thousand years ago. It is still true today.

Now what on earth could management have to do with virtue?

Well, in order to answer this question one would have to write a whole book! This book, for example.

This book is a dream of how to do it right, of how to play a fair game, and of what might happen if we did. It is about the creation of happiness. It is about how to organise life in a decent way to make ideas become reality.

It is within the power of individuals to create their own happiness, or unhappiness as the case may be. It all depends on visions and goals, on their ethical quality. It also depends on organisational dexterity.

As this book describes ideal states of performance and co-operation, it may appear initially unreal. However, there is a hope that one day it will be made real.

Let us work on it.

1

Everybody a Manager

What is management? What is a manager? Something special perhaps? A select type of person?

Neither of the two. "Management" is a plain English word, and to manage something is a plain thing to do. "To manage" means: to get something done. For example: "She manages her household well." – "He manages a corner shop." – "We managed to get home before the rain." Born managers all of them, no question!

The word is derived from the Italian *maneggiare* and that again from the Latin root *manus agere*, and that means: to act with one's hands. It follows that managers are people who can give a hand when a job needs doing. They are people who can make ideas come true.

A manager makes sure that work gets done, either by doing it himself, or by getting others to do it.

A manager puts ideas into practice.

Some people have brilliant ideas and cannot put them into practice. They simply are not managers; they do not have that gift.

Could any worker be a manager? Any employee? Any housewife? When they can put ideas into practice, yes. When they can only follow orders, no.

There are two significant points: firstly, that a person has ideas; secondly, that he or she is prepared to take responsibility for putting them into practice.

To the extent that this happens, this person is a manager.

It all begins with a thought

A manager has ideas, as stated. He also puts them into practice; he realises them. He obtains results. He starts something, works on it, and completes it.

In the beginning, there is a thought. This is followed by activity. At the end: a result. Thought – activity – result: these three components form what can be described as a Performance Package.

A Performance Package begins with a thought, an idea, a concept. It ends with a result or product. In order to make it happen one needs energy: willpower, muscular force, steam, electricity, whatever is required.

The three components of a Performance Package: thought – activity – result.

A Performance Package does not simply occur "by itself". It has a beginning and an ending. And, most importantly, it has someone intending it.

Which means: Anything that happens in the world of human societies is intended by someone or other.

Conversely: even when nothing happens in an area (although circumstances are screaming for something to be done), there is still an underlying intention. Even omitted action begins with a thought.

Each thought leads to a result. Each intention has its consequence – provided one was to put the idea into practice; provided one added energy to the thought and acted upon it.

Only a thought that was never attempted to be realised is entirely without consequences.

Thus a Performance Package brings about a result. But not all results are good results. They could be bad results; they could be mere "half-dones". No matter; as soon as one has acted, some result is obtained, inevitably.

Not all actions are sensible; some are confused, perverted or evil. This is because they are based on confused, perverted or evil thoughts.

Thoughts are abstract. They exist only in the mind, nowhere else. Results are concrete. They exist in the real world. A result one can experience, touch, see, smell, hear, taste. There is proof of it.

So be aware: the moment you add energy to a thought you have to be prepared to take responsibility.

Organisation and leadership

On the way from abstract thought to concrete result, energies are activated, and materials are moved about. This happens in a certain space and takes a certain amount of time. There is panting, sweating and cursing, and one gets the occasional bruise. Lack of room and pressing time targets are routinely part of this activity.

None of this happens in one's mind; none of this is abstract. This is the real world. In order to make those activities run along orderly lines, one has to organise them.

Organisation means efficiently co-ordinating Performance Packages in order to obtain a desired end result.

This is truly the art of management. Nothing is to be left incomplete; nothing is to be done twice. All forces, finances, resources and tools are to be used optimally. Efficiency is the trump card in the pack. Waste one cannot afford.

Planning, financial budgeting, and computer-designed future scenarios are unquestionable elements of organisation, but good leadership of team members and colleagues is the most essential element.

After all it is the people who do the work. And when they do not feel like it, one can close the shop down. Game over!

Listless team members are unmotivated. They have no motive to play the game any further. They see no reason to move anything. They do nothing.

Even though a game, on paper, may have been worked out down to its most minute details, without well-motivated team members it will not even get started.

Leadership is the art of keeping team members interested in the game and making them give their best.

Honest leadership means that management is in personal contact with its team members, understands and respects them, and makes them feel part of the game as a whole. When management knows how to lead people in this fashion it will obtain very good results.

In order to get results quickly one could of course force people or mislead them by trickery and treachery. One could bribe, use brutal means or crafty betrayals. That is, however, not honest leadership. It is an attempt to take away people's self-determinism and enslave them.

This book does not cover any such measures. It deals with honest leadership on the basis of free will and self-determinism for all participants.

On the nature of a good manager

A manager is a leader. In full view of all the obstacles it is the leader who has to keep motivating everybody, including himself.

Anyone found motivating others will naturally be looked at as a leader.

Who has leadership ability? Someone with a quick and easy

grasp of situations. Someone who gives a good example, does not lose sight of the end result to be obtained, and who inspires courage and morale in his team mates. Someone who, despite all willpower and rigour, still understands their personal difficulties. Someone who stays incorruptible.

(*On gendering: Women and men are equally good managers without question. So it goes without saying that any "him" or "his" in this text should immediately be followed by a "her" or "hers", except that this would make the text harder to read.)

A good manager is approachable and friendly:

He can listen. A good manager never has "no time".

He understands the tight spot a team mate might be in. He does not end a talk until this is resolved.

He recognises and respects the emotional situation of his partners. He does not go across their feelings like a steamroller.

He comprehends the difficulties of his team mates from *their* viewpoint. And he respects them for that, rather than ridiculing them, or deriding them.

A good manager is competent:

He commands excellent professional knowledge and a wealth of practical experience.

He is decisive, and willing to take responsibility for the consequences of his decisions.

He can demonstrably control Performance Packages. He can knowingly and willingly start, perform and stop a Performance Package.

He enjoys his work and has the courage to take a risk.

Furthermore, a good manager is dedicated to the goals, ideals and plans of his group and does not lose sight of them. He is loyal.

He uses his friendliness to motivate his team mates. He uses his competence to find solutions. He never gives up.

It is his responsibility to take the initial idea to a good end result. It is also up to everybody in the team, but it is up to him more than to anybody else.

He knows, when he lets his head hang low, the game is over. Therefore, he does not let his head hang low. Regardless of his personal views and feelings, he keeps his poise.

A leader has poise: incorruptibility, integrity, and ethics.

The human condition: being, doing, and having

Above we referred to the Performance Package in terms of thought – activity – result.

In order to realise an idea, one would, as a leader, have to be able to look at it from the viewpoint of those whose role is to put it into practice, and of those who are going to be affected by this. If one does not do this, the idea will be "above the level of life". It will have little connection with the actual reality of life.

One would have to be willing to put oneself into the shoes of the person on the job and visualise his point of view. One would have to be willing *to be* him and see life from his angle. (This could be defined as compassion.)

Furthermore, one would have to be able to preview the entire Performance Package from the viewpoint of the person whose role is to execute it. One would have to be willing *to do* it in that way.

And finally, one would have to be fully aware of one's end product and be willing to obtain it. One would have to be willing *to have* a definite result.

The willingness to be, the willingness to do, and the willingness to have are the three fundamental conditions of human existence.

8

Those who are weak in any of these areas will soon drown – in life as well as in management.

Example: "The baker bakes bread." "Bread" is what you are willing to have; it is the end product. "Baking" is what you must be willing to do to have bread. "A baker" is what you must be willing to be.

In order to have bread, one must do something, namely bake it. In order to bake, one must be something, namely a baker.

One does not have to be a baker by trade in order to bake some bread, but one must be willing to play the role of a baker at least until that particular loaf of bread is done.

You cannot have a result without doing something first. Yet you cannot do anything without accepting a certain role or function. And for that, you have to be willing to be someone. That and only that is the prerequisite for any game in life, and indeed for the game of life.

Example: A playground in the park. An elderly gentleman with a dog watches the children at play. The dog uses the opportunity to do his poo in the children's sandbox. The mothers present are rightfully disgusted. They ask the man to remove the dog's turd. His face turns red: "What??? You people think I'm the street cleaner?"

A street cleaner he does not wish to be. This is beneath him. Therefore no doing (no cleaning up), therefore no having (no clean sandbox). The turd stays where it is.

Even though one may be in principle *willing* to be, do, or have something, one might still be incapable of actually *executing* it properly, and take that particular Performance Package to a successful end result. This is the difference between intention and action. Actually getting the product in the end is quite different from merely intending it. "I only meant well" is no excuse for a blunder.

The intention of course is the starting point; this is always the case. Therefore, even though one might fail, one has at least been

9

trying, and that in itself deserves to be recognised.

A particular result (a having) can always be obtained in more than one way. Anyone who is determined to really achieve or obtain something will have no problems with being or doing. He will accept any route and any identity, as long as it takes him in the right direction.

Being and doing fall into place all by themselves provided one keeps the desired end result firmly in mind and reacts flexibly to the ever changing environment.

How being, doing, and having can be a problem

Of the three basic prerequisites of human existence, the willingness to have is the most difficult to build up and retain.

To *be* somebody – no problem. A mental experiment, no more. Totally abstract. Does not hurt at all. You could easily dream yourself into being just anyone: tinker, tailor, soldier, sailor.

To *do* something – that is more real than being. It may take a few skills, and perhaps some effort, but still it is no problem. Because as long as nobody looks at the actual effects that you have created, the doing stays comfortably inconsequential.

But *having* something – that is where it becomes serious. Because results are concrete as well as consequential. They refer back to oneself. Always. No excuses.

Some people refuse to play a certain role, be it only for a short duration. They do not like to take on a certain way of being, a certain identity. They fear it might be beneath them.

Others have absolutely no problem with thinking their way into all types of roles and identities, but the moment it comes to actually doing something, they feel stalled. They can mentally assume each and every type of being, but the respective doing just never seems to spring forth.

Such people love to dream of pies in the sky. They develop future visions and sell bits of blue sky to people. The sort of stuff they dream of being! You would not believe it. And of course it has to be tomorrow. Except – nothing ever seems to happen. No doing.

Others again manage to perform, but they lose sight of having to produce a certain something at the end. Getting a proper result as the purpose of the whole activity is an idea which gets lost on the way. They do and do and do, they race from one appointment to the next, they appear at ten different important events at the same time, they are all over the place, they are terribly important – and there is absolutely no result. No having.

The reward for being, doing, and having

As important as it is to actually obtain results, many people still do not get paid for the quality and quantity of their actual products. They do not get rewarded for the result of their performance. Often they are simply paid for their doing, no matter what they achieve. The main criterion for getting paid is: having looked convincingly busy for a number of hours. (This was certainly true until recently, but fortunately it is increasingly changing in the work-world to payment by result.)

Some people are honoured just for their being. They are rewarded for what they represent. In the past they, or perhaps their forefathers, have produced valuable products: for example as kings, artists, industrialists, or sports champions. In the past they were a somebody. For as long as they can draw from the glory of their past, they still represent something. They have a valuable being. To be associated with that sort of being appears so important to some folks that they pay money for it.

Could work be a game?

Work or game? What is the difference?

Work is often associated with enforcement, bad temper and stress. A game on the other hand is usually considered fun and a personal challenge. One works because one has to; one plays because one likes to.

Now let us take for example some football pros: they have got it made, haven't they, because they play all the time. Or do they in fact work? Hours and hours of training, day in, day out, aching muscles, bruises, competitions, the press...

Stress as far as the eye can see – is that work or play?

"I play the violin in a symphony orchestra, but it can be quite a dreadful routine." – "I am an actress with top contracts, but some film directors I could just kill!" – "I work in a post office at the counter, and I love to see all the people from this neighbourhood and have a chat with them." – "I am a professional tennis player, but after a day at the tennis court I feel knackered." – "I'm a nurse, and I do night shifts a lot, which is hard, but I just love to help."

Do you consider your marital partner a co-worker or a co-player? The members of your sports club – are they co-workers or co-players? Your business partner who you plan the future with – is he a co-worker or a co-player?

Whether at work, in the family, during concert rehearsals, or at a tennis tournament – everybody tries to win and gives his best; everybody wants to make wishes come true. Everybody invests their strength, skill and cleverness, some more, some less.

When you are successful, no matter whether you are working or playing, your power knows no limits. You muster unthought-of energies. You are proud of yourself and look with great expectations at your future.

However, when obstacles become insurmountable, when success no longer occurs, when losses gain the upper hand, one feels depressed and unhappy.

What work and play have in common is this: goals, obstacles and freedoms.

Goals must be known as well as realistic and attainable. One must have personally and freely agreed to them.

Obstacles must be of such magnitude that they constitute interesting challenges, but they must also be surmountable.

Freedoms one must have in order to play creatively and bring one's personality to bear. Too many rules, too tight a leadership make one feel suffocated.

A game is fun when goals, obstacles and freedoms are well balanced. Players are then permitted to put themselves out creatively. They overcome unforeseen challenges, and see themselves progressing towards their goal. Then what you give and what you get are well in proportion with each other. That is flying; that is real happiness. In this situation work becomes a game.

According to the dictionary, the word "work" often implies labour and toil. There is hardship connected with it. And indeed the moment goals are impressed on one by force, the moment obstacles are too large to be overcome, the moment one loses one's freedoms, a game ceases to be fun. It turns into work in the bad sense of the word. It becomes a pain.

In this book we shall use the word "game" for human activities. No matter what activity, not matter whether it feels good or bad, we shall call it a game. Taking a walk, running a company, studying to get one's PhD, getting married – these are some of the games people play.

The art of living

The art of living consists on the one hand of being able to consciously assume a certain type of being (a role, an office, a post, an identity like boss or father), and on the other hand of the ability to let go of it again. Once you get so deeply entangled in a specific type of being which you can no longer discard, life becomes a drag.

When you are actively engaged in a game, and at the same time keep a position outside the game, that game will not be able to affect you. Such a player stands detached. He keeps a remote viewpoint.

Never forget: you are above and beyond all the roles you are playing. Because you are the cause of their existence.

All these roles can only exist because you have agreed to their existence. Perhaps under duress, certainly, but nevertheless you have agreed. Therefore, at the moment you can turn the "I have to" into an "I want to", you have won.

Psychosomatic illnesses and neuroses begin to show when you refuse to accept the various roles and games of your life, when you resist them and in consequence feel pressurised by them. Equally you can get ill when you, for fear of loss, do not dare to let go of those roles and games.

Either way your thoughts will be caught in incomplete Performance Packages of the past, present and future. For this reason you will not be disposed to fully concentrate on the game at hand. You will not be in the Here & Now. You will feel overwhelmed, stressed, and eventually become ill.

The remedy: turn refusal into acceptance. Recall the original moment of agreement. Look at it, review it and take the emotional charge out of it. That will free you up to change conditions.

The team: founders, players, pieces

Players are people who know the rules, agree with them, and abide by them. They are disciplined, decision-happy and courageous.

Yet on a playing field you find not only players, but also pieces.

Pieces are like the pawn, rook, bishop, knight, queen and king on the chessboard. They are pushed around. They act as they are told. They do not ask questions. They do not know what the players have in mind. They have no view of the whole game.

Some of these pieces are broken pieces. They are beaten. They did not make it. They lie about at the edge of the playing field.

Games are created by games founders. A games founder envisions goals and ideals for the group. His visions inspire the game and its players.

A games founder knows the rightness and importance of his visions with great inner certainty. He does not doubt them in any way. Often he feels in connection with a spiritual power source which gives him the energy to work through the hard parts and to overcome all obstacles.

From the power which the game founder represents, the game players also draw. Even when the founder died a long time ago, he in the opinion of the players constitutes the bridge between themselves and that source of power.

In the eyes of the players, the founder never dies. Examples of this are benign politicians such as kings or presidents, the founders of traditional companies, the instigators of religions, and also mythical heroes and demigods.

Management: life on a tightrope

Between founder and players stands management. Management is the link between the founder's ideas and the activities of the players.

Management develops game rules, and ensures that they are adhered to. Game rules ideally further the progress of the game and pave the way towards the vision.

The attitude of the players towards management is different from their attitude to the game founder. The founder is forever popular. People love him. He lives as the radiant star in the night sky, as the eternal giver of impulses. The players generally find it easy to honour and respect him (particularly when the founder is long dead).

Management, conversely, is likely to become the target of hate and scorn from the side of game players. For management acts with severity. It demands, drives, punishes. Players find it very easy to get angry and resentful.

Game players feel deeply loyal towards the game founder. They share his visions, and from these visions they draw their power and hope. This is the energy on which the whole game runs.

Game players trust management only while it makes decisions which, in the opinion of the players, contribute towards the achievement of the goals and ideals represented by the founder.

Therefore management, seen as the link between founder and players, draws its energy from this live wire, from this current of vital energy. It can only exist and act as long as it is empowered by the players.

Any time that management makes decisions which appear to be deviating from the founder's vision, the players become suspicious. They ask questions. When these remain unanswered, there is frustration, sabotage, strike, mutiny, rebellion, civil war, terrorism.

How bad management can degrade a game

For management to dominate rather than serve a game, it must secretly occupy the position of the game founder. For this purpose it is convenient when the game founder is long dead since dead founders do not protest. Further, such a management must turn players into pieces, and make them act on enforced commands rather than their self-determinism. The only players then left will sit in management. They have hijacked the game and made it their own.

This is how a treacherous management might degrade players, and turn them into pieces:

It could glorify the late game founder, yet cleverly pervert and distort his goals and ideals for the benefit of management. This way it is suggested to the players that things are still as they always were and that they are not in a new game when in actual fact they are (i.e. in that of the corrupt management).

Conversely, a treacherous management could spread a blanket of silence over the old game, and severely punish any mentioning of the old game. It could erase the name of the late founder, burn his writings, and have itself proclaimed the new game founder.

Furthermore a treacherous management could withhold vital documents on the nature of the game. It could make decisions and not give any reasons. It could replace sensible rules by unsubstantiated arbitrary regulations. It could generate uncertainty and fear in the players. It could punish free thought and only reward parroting the dogma. It could enforce the game, and suppress each aspect of fun. It would permit players to communicate with each other only on the level of pieces, thus making it all appear very democratic, but would deny the existence of the real players, of the actual game masters behind the curtain.

A strong team with able players knows its enemies, can name them, and fight them. It looks expectantly into its future.

A weak, degraded team, which consists mainly of game pieces and some broken pieces, usually is run from behind the scenes by anonymous unknown wire-pullers. Such a team does not know its enemies, and so cannot fight them. Such a team sees no future. It stares into its past, thinks about it, and indulges in self-reproach.

Such extreme examples demonstrate the defeat of a team, and the end of what perhaps once started as a very worthwhile game.

2

Creating the Future

The previous chapter demonstrated a Performance Package as consisting of three component parts: thought – energy and action – result. The prerequisite for good success in the execution of a Performance Package was recognised as being the willingness to be, to do, and to have.

This chapter addresses the development of concepts. A concept is a clear idea of what and how one intends to achieve something. It means to mentally pre-empt a Performance Package.

Concepts and ideals

We have probably all recognised the experience where the only thing that happens is what one has conceived earlier. Nothing else. So when you think in a blurry or wrong way, you will get blurry or wrong results. Any time you do not consider certain things, mistakes will creep in at exactly these spots. Therefore making a clear concept is enormously important.

Never act on a vague thought running through your head as it might not have any bearing on reality. Intuition is fine and important and has its place, but it is not sufficient. A good Game Concept implies that you can mentally imagine its realisation in all detail: "What is the product of our project going to look like? What is going to happen once it is out in the world?"

We are referring to images, not vague thoughts. When you see images in your mind, when vivid pictures come streaming in, that is the beginning stage of a true Game Concept. (How to formulate a Game Concept in full is covered in a later section of this chapter.)

Brainstorming and Mind Mapping are therefore very useful

to stimulate one's imagination. Ideas whirl around, pies are placed in the sky, mountains are moved. All very well. But to get down to earth one needs to take it further. One needs a concept that contains answers to all the details of being, doing and having: What exactly is to be produced? Who is to do it? How should it be done? Until when?

If these questions were left unanswered the game would disappear in smoke before it was even started.

An example: Father says: "Let's buy a house!", and the whole family shouts hooray. Everybody is enthusiastic.

At this moment there are as many houses as heads, because everybody sees his own dreams before his eyes.

If one started acting now, each person would make plans and get information on the house he personally imagines. And each person might still think he or she was acting in accordance with everybody else.

Nobody asks for the purpose and intent of Father's idea. What did he have in mind when he suggested buying a house? So the central question which needs asking would be: "For what purpose should we buy a house?"

As this question was not openly asked and discussed at the dinner table, everybody found their personal answer to it. The daughter wanted a bungalow by the sea (to go swimming), Father a hunter's lodge in the forest (to go hunting), Mother a cottage out in the country (to do gardening). So everybody dreams their own dreams, and acts accordingly.

Individual desires were not blended with each other. There was certainly an overall agreement that a house should be bought – but not what for, not what type of house! And so each of them could happily continue dreaming his own dreams.

What was missing here is an exact agreement regarding the original idea: "What exact house do we want to buy?" There is just no way around sharing this and agreeing on it.

All individual desires must be fitted under one lid. That lid is the ideal state everybody can agree to, and feels motivated towards. That is the core of your Game Concept.

It may require a great deal of communication to get there, but that is worth it. Raising dreams to the level of full consciousness keeps people from waking up to some big devastating disappointment when it is too late.

We are powered by dreams

The lesson to be learnt from the above is this: an ideal state that is relevant to all participants must be found and formulated. An ideal state which everybody can agree with wholeheartedly, and would strive to attain. Nobody will move one finger without an ideal state, a vision, a dream.

Ideals are the motor behind all human endeavours.

Why does one do anything at all? Because one hopes that he or she will feel better afterwards. One does not feel satisfied with the way things are at present; one strives for greater dimensions. What they are is different for everybody.

Take our example of buying a house: "Why do we actually need a house?" On the surface this is asking for a practical purpose. But on a deeper level it is pointing at an ideal state behind it, at the dream, the vision: "We want to have a rose garden and a big dog. And there should be a horse-riding area nearby; and a swimming pool."

None of this is practical. It is dream stuff.

In order to realise an ideal state, you need to envision it vividly. How you are going to live and work and eat and sleep in your future house? A colourful vision is what this needs to be; it has to touch one's emotions. You must be able to see and feel and taste it.

The ideal state envisioned by you conveys the idea of the pleasure you will have in the future. This way you will never forget what you are aiming towards.

The ideal state is your navigator into the future.

Given full certainty regarding your dream, you will know which course to steer even when your boat is rocked about by a storm. It is from this certainty that hope and the power to persist derive.

Everybody has his desires and wishes to see them fulfilled. For that he puts himself out; for nothing else. This does not mean to say that all desires would be life enhancing – not at all! Many desires are destructive to man, beast and nature, and some (like extremist sports) are even suicidal. Still, they make one feel better – because there surely is some ideal state behind it, otherwise people would not want to have it that way.

When recognising the totality of all the wishes of a person, you have his ideal state regarding life. According to that he will aim to arrange life for himself. This is just as true for individuals as for families, groups, and races.

One could certainly be of differing opinions about the value of some visions. A cannibal would regard a man in the same way that a cook looks at a chicken. "A nice and crunchy human thigh" is to the cannibal just as attractive an ideal as "a nice and crunchy chicken thigh" for the ordinary citizen. The victims naturally reserve opinions of their own. This goes to show that not all ideal states appeal to everybody.

Only very few people have clarity on their personal dreams. Try it out: ask someone. You will quite rarely get an authentic reply. You will get to hear superficial stuff picked up from television, yes, but rarely something authentic. This is because ideals quite often exist as tacit agreements only. They are not discussed. Yet although they may be unconscious, or perhaps unreflected upon, they still determine the creation of life to the highest extent.

What a single person, a family, a race or a culture considers good and right, quite often is not documented. You only begin to recognise the existence of such ideals at the moment you happen to transgress against one of them, and then feel the consequences.

Unconscious, unspoken ideals, taken as a matter of course by the community, are an emotional powder keg. If utilised properly by a manager, this powder keg works like a fuel unit giving a team the driving force of a missile. But if handled carelessly, the emotional discharge going along with its release may blow the team up and perhaps the whole game with it!

It is therefore sensible to put the ideal state openly on the table for all players to know it, share it, and desire it. In such a case, each and every one is fully prepared to fill no matter what post, and do any activity, be it high or low.

In such a case there is absolutely no problem with being and doing. Because the desire to have is always senior.

Players play along as long as they are able. They hope that one day their dreams will become reality. Out of this hope they draw their power. As long as the game follows the right direction, be it even in small steps, this power source will never cease. As long as there is hope, the game will continue on.

Each success, each piece of good news will lift the morale of the players and incite them to even higher activity. But if the hopes are disappointed for too long a time, the players will feel exhausted. They will become depressed and ill.

Each goal is attainable, each ideal state can be fulfilled, as long as they are realistic, and as long as there is sufficient willpower to back them up. It may take more than one lifetime, more than one generation. But do not lose your patience.

"We'll get it done, no matter what!" This is the mark of quality of a good leader.

How to get things done

So far we have been considering what we want to have as a result of a game. We were looking at purposes and ideal states. Of the three conditions of human existence only the having has so far been fully addressed. The question: "How are we going to do it?" has not yet been asked. We were not quite at that point yet. The players were still too busy formulating their goals, wishes and ideals concisely and conclusively.

The power for the doing is generated by a person's will. If his intention is clear, his doing will have direction. Therefore willing comes before doing. Willing is anchored in the being of a person.

Without being there is no doing; without doing there is no having. But even though a player's willpower may be absolutely focused, the doing still is not fully predictable. Why? Because he is not the only one on the playing field.

Apart from you and your team there are competing players and teams that need to be considered. They all strive ahead, and some of them may be actually hostile.

Additionally, one encounters all sort of obstacles in one's working materials: splintering wood, bursting concrete, overheating gadgets, computer malfunction.

These obstacles can be very hard to predict. Nevertheless, nothing works without far-sighted planning. Far-sighted planning means: you think your way into all possible eventualities. This allows you to have answers ready when needed.

We surely are no prophets, but to go along improvising since "one does not know the future anyway", would put one at the mercy of the winds of fate.

Levels of action

So let us consider levels of action, and let us give them a ranking. For lack of better words let us consider that a plan is the senior level of action, that each plan contains several programs, each program several projects, and each project several orders.

In order to reach a goal, one needs a *plan* (or several of them).

In order to execute one particular plan, one has to divide it up into separate steps: these are the *programs*.

In order to execute programs, one has to divide them up into separate steps: these are the *projects*.

In order to execute projects, one has to divide them up into separate steps: these are the *orders*.

Each order has its predetermined, defined result. The results of various individual orders add up to the end result of a project. The results of individual projects add up to the end result of a specific program. The results of individual programs add up to the end result of a plan. The results of individual plans add up to an end result which one might call "goal attained".

And if, in the course of time, the majority of these goals were attained, one might actually come close to a situation of reality matching the ideal state. That would be the end result of the whole game, the fulfilment of its purpose. End of game. Could not get any better.

Goals and visions: the difference

A vision is not a goal; a goal not a vision. The difference is this: a goal is situated on a material plane. A vision, a dream, an ideal state – these are situated on a spiritual plane. "Freedom" for example is a vision; so are "independence", "health", "happiness" etc. Most visions are built on the basis of virtues.

Goals are production targets on a pragmatic level.
Visions are ideal states on a spiritual level.

To give an example: If you, as a political prisoner, dreamed of freedom, you would have as a first goal: knock down the guard and get the key. The next goal would be: open the prison door and run to a safe address. The goal after that: see to it that you are taken out of the country. Then: be granted asylum in a neutral country. To achieve each of these goals a lot of plans, programs, projects, and orders would be needed. Eventually, once you became a free man, reality would be matching your vision. That would end the game called "attaining freedom". The name of the new game would be: "enjoy your freedom and do something with it".

Spontaneity? – Yes, please!

With all this planning and predetermination of goals and products, is there still room for spontaneity? Oh yes, there is. Indeed, spontaneity is a vital ingredient. Because no plan, no program, no project, no order can pre-empt all possible eventualities which may occur on the actual work site.

One must be prepared for anything. Alertness and the readiness to act are the mark of a good player. He is acting now-now-now, always in the present moment.

Part of that is that he thinks the necessary Performance Package through to its end in order to have it down pat at the word "Go!" It should be in the back of his mind at any given moment.

All one's power is now. There is no other point in time to exert it.

The doing must be flexible. It has to immediately adapt to the constantly changing conditions of the environment. It has to be spontaneous. Not chaotic – spontaneous! A vast difference.

Good rules will keep you out of trouble

What sort of doing is the correct one? That which is conducive to the attainment of the goals and ideals to which one feels committed. Otherwise it is not.

When everybody does what they privately think is right, there is anarchy. Literally this means "a state with no order". It's the opposite of "hierarchy" which means "holy order" (both taken from the Greek).

A hierarchy does not have to be vertical and dictatorial, quite the contrary! For order to be "holy" you need no system of a dictator at the top and his minions below him, but rather very awake players in small teams who are sworn in to their goals and ideals, and where everybody is equal to everybody else. In the best possible hierarchy a game would be played on the basis of telepathic communication alone.

In larger groups with many players and complex tasks it is unavoidable to channel the doing along pre-designed routes. Otherwise there is chaos. So you will need rules, game rules.

Rules put down the conditions under which the game happens. They are the answer to the question: "What are we going by when we act?"

Rules define the playing field in the minds of the players.

"What must be? What should be? What should not be under any circumstances? What may one do? What must one never do? How is one to do it, and when?" And so on.

Those who know the rules understand what they are to do and not to do.

Rules constitute the governing criteria for the being, doing and having of the players. They describe and order the positions and ranks of players (their being), their performance amongst each other and within the production process (their doing), and the nature, quality and quantity of their products and results (their having).

Instead of "game rules", one might say just as well: guidelines, policies, principles, laws, edicts, constitutions, agreements, contracts.

Rules which make the goals and ideals of the group appear

attainable are accepted by players as sensible. Such rules create a feeling of safety and stability.

Sensible rules channel game activities towards the attainment of goals and ideals.

Rules which do not channel the being, doing and having of players in the direction of the goals and ideals of the game are not sensible. They need to be either altered or removed.

Those who act spontaneously within the framework of sensible rules, and thereby instigate the game, will always find recognition. Such players do not feel glued to the letter of the law. Quite the contrary: they act freely and creatively – and still do not violate the rules!

Mentally, in his being, a spontaneous player has grasped the concept of the game. This is why he can smoothly realise it in his doing. By fully exploring the freedoms provided by the rules he attains excellent results (his having).

There are also those who slavishly stick to instructions, who, lacking the faintest spark of personal comprehension or inspiration, are seen walking about with a book of regulations under their arm, quoting from it at every opportunity. Such people contort the real purpose of game rules. They view the rules as more important than the game, and furthermore, assume themselves more important than the game. They pull the brakes, slowing the game down.

Such pompousness does not always immediately become apparent, because at first glance the person seems to be acting "correctly". Yet the effects of such "correctness" do make it obvious what is happening.

There is a third type: those who due to lack of information or out of mischief transgress against the rules, be it openly or covertly.

Handling the third type is actually easier than handling the pompous fellow. The uninformed can be corrected. The chaos merchants one would remove from the playing field (by taking their licence to participate away, by putting them into jail, whatever). The pompous ones, however, are a serious problem as they fail to grasp the point of your criticism, because they are ever so right.

Rules may change; visions must stay

It is unavoidable, as well as vital, that game rules must be reviewed at times. Circumstances change, and so game rules must be adapted to them.

Antiquated game rules lead to outdated decisions. Circumstances do change, yes, and with them the requirements for the doing, and for this reason the rules need adjusting – but the goals, and even more so the ideals of the game, must be kept intact under all circumstances!

If one changed goals and ideals one would alienate the whole game. If this was done clandestinely, such as by a treacherous management, one would in the end wind up in a different game than in the beginning – and it might even go by unnoticed.

Rules need to be changed, yes, yet goals and ideals must remain. Goals and ideals are like a lighthouse on the horizon. If they are tampered with, the lighthouse will disappear from the horizon.

Only products tell the tale

Now the game we have prepared for so thoroughly has begun. Ideals, goals, and rules have been established; plans have been made, and separated into programs and projects. Everybody has their orders and is busily working.

This results in products. Products are unavoidably attained by any human activity, be it industrial, household, sports, gardening or farming. They do not exclusively exist in the form of material objects. Improved conditions and acquired skills are also the result of human activity; they are also products.

In principle this has nothing to do with goodness or badness. A polite child for example is a product of good upbringing. A brilliantly performed piano piece is the product of lots of practice. Traffic jams are the product of bad traffic planning. Environmental problems are the product of badly thought-out industrialisation. Products are products. How to judge them in terms of ethical value is a separate issue.

Products are the result of a Performance Package, regardless of whether it was completed or interrupted. They are not what somebody happens to be *doing* at a given moment. They are what is left *after* the doing is finished. They are what you have as a consequence of your doing.

This simple principle is generally not recognised. Take for example building a house. We ask the bricklayer about his product. He says: "I build walls." The carpenter: "I put the timbers up for the roof." The tiler: "I cover the walls and floors of bathrooms with tiles."

None of them have described their actual product. They all have answered with what they are doing.

A product is not what you do. It is what you have.

Expressed in terms of having, our tradesmen should have said: "My product is a solid, vertical wall." – "The properly and firmly set timber frame of the roof." "The faultlessly and evenly tiled bathroom."

The prerequisite for this would be the "willingness to have" described in the first chapter. A very uncomfortable prerequisite indeed! For it demands a large sense of responsibility; it demands much more responsibility than the willingness to do.

By merely doing-doing-doing you can easily make a good impression. But when it comes to the actual having, when you have to present something visible and tangible, that is different.

That really demands a clear vision, strong willingness, and a large sense of responsibility.

When you are in the middle of the doing it feels endless. There is a danger of becoming immersed in all that doing. Doing, doing, doing – it seems to have no beginning and no end. This can put one into a trance. One loses sight of the general picture and the ultimate purpose. It might even take one down to the point of despair.

People who only see what they are currently doing without any attention on what has been done already (on the having obtained) quite often feel haunted and nervous. They are "stressed". Psychosomatic illnesses can be a consequence.

Such people have a problem with products. Products are real; they are there to be seen and touched. There is factual evidence for them. People who talk a lot about their products, or are "ever so busy" attaining them, instead of simply presenting them, have none. It is just hot-air talk.

How do you judge products and their quality? Here is a principle: Look at facts. Do not listen to opinions.

Look! Do not just listen.

When we say, "A product is the result of a Performance Package, whether complete or incomplete", we mean any type of result, not only the model of perfection. We also mean the half-complete job which was left abandoned; we mean the useless outcome, even the dangerous outcome. A product is a product; it is what you have left on the work bench after you have quit the job for that day, whether half-done, fully done, valuable or worthless. It is what is there.

When is a product considered valuable? When it stands in accordance with the ideal state to which it is supposed to contribute. Its value is judged in terms of the ideal state to which it paves the way. The more a product falls in line with the ideal state envisioned, the more it helps one come closer to that ideal state, the more valuable will that product be considered.

A product that does not help to approximate the ideal state envisioned is worthless.

For valuable products you get exchange: acknowledgements, recognition, support, money. For worthless products you get nothing, except perhaps blame, ridicule, even punishment.

Money is not a product, by the way. It is only the exchange for the products one has handed out. The stock market is the only place in the world where this is different: there they make money out of money with no product in between. So-called "finance products" are just money made directly out of money. You cannot touch them; they are not real.

Selling and buying dreams

An end product consists of a number of sub-products. An example of a sub-product: a well-played ball in soccer. A further sub-product: a ball that went into the goal of the other team.

Example of an end product: more goals shot than the opposing team, having won the game. Exchange: recognition, medals, sponsoring, advertising contracts.

The players of a given game, as well as anyone affected by that game, will judge the quality of sub-products and end products in terms of their correspondence with the ideal state for that game.

Sub-products contribute to the end product, yet by themselves they have little value. You do not get any exchange for them; you cannot sell them. End products, however, apart from being a source of pride to the producer, also have material value for him in that he can get the end products of other teams in exchange for them, or sell them for money to a customer.

This works only as long as the customer also considers this product valuable. Why would he? Because of the imaginary value the product holds for him. In order to be interesting to a buyer, the product must relate to some desired ideal state in the mind of the buyer. Only on this condition will a buyer be prepared to give an exchange for it.

The moment the customer decides to buy, the imaginary value of an end product ranks a lot higher in his eyes than its mere practical value. For the buyer to part with his money he must consider the product to be good and useful with respect to the fulfilment of his personal dreams. If the product does not appear promising with respect to the fulfilment of the customer's desires, if it does not seem to move him closer to his envisioned ideal state, he will not buy it.

People do not buy what they practically need.
They buy the fulfilment of their dreams.

This is even true for the choice of such trivial goods as for example the materials used in building a house. One does not simply buy any old brick, heating system, or insulation materials. No way! One buys stability, durability, safety, economical efficiency, and a desired external appearance, meaning beauty.

A product that is considered by a customer so valuable that he is prepared to give an exchange for it, we shall call in this text a Final Exchangeable Product.

Important: Not every Final Exchangeable Product is also ethically valuable. It may have market value but that is not to say that it would also be ethically valuable. So to be very distinct on our definitions: When we say "exchangeable" we are only referring to the worth of a product in the eyes of the marketplace. We do not mean to imply that the ethical consequences in the context of the production or use of a Final Exchangeable Product are ethically acceptable. (See also the chapter on Ethics.)

Is it going the right way?

How is one to judge whether or not the right direction is being followed? Some game cycles take a very long time. They can last years, decades, or even generations. Statistics are the answer.

Statistics permit the comparison of today with yesterday and the prediction of tomorrow.

"Last summer we had more rain than this year." – Not a statistic, merely a subjective guess.

"Last week we used up a good truckload full of concrete; that's nearly twice as much as two weeks ago." – "In this river you'll find fewer fish every year." – Raw estimates, nothing more.

Raw estimates and subjective guesses permit judging a situation, yet they are not really statistics. Statistics are precise. They define in terms of exact figures what has been achieved. They measure observable performances during a defined time period. They "quantify" an operation in that they define the decrease or increase of observable quantities as a measurement of its progress.

How many centimetres of rain per square metre did you get last summer, and how many this summer? How many cubic metres of concrete were used up last week, and how many this week? How many pikes, carps and eels were caught during the fishing season in a given section of the river this year, in comparison to last year? These are statistics, not guesses.

Tendency up or down? That's what it is all about. When statistics are formulated sensibly, their up-or-down tendency gives a direct clue to the direction of the game. Does it move towards the ideal state or does it not?

Statistics are formulated on the principle: "The more or, respectively, the less a certain observation can be made, the more it goes in the right direction."

That is true for everything, even for one's love life: Last month, did you get any fewer kisses, chocolates, and roses than two months ago?

Players should be judged by their statistics and not only by the cultured way they express or dress themselves. The less cultured ones with good statistics are the better players. They achieve something.

Look! Do not listen!

How to set up a successful game

With the steps below you will be formulating a Game Concept for each and every possible game, be it large or small. The Game Concept enables you to work it out in any dimension, monitor it, and take it to a successful conclusion.

Step 1 – the Vision: Where are we heading?

To which "impossible dream" do you aspire? What would you like to see happen?

What situations for yourself or people involved do you imagine? What states of life, mind and body do you desire? What is life going to look like when the dream has come true, after the work has been done?

Describe what you see. Describe the images of the future coming to mind. Don't describe what you think. Describe what you see and feel. It has to make you smile! If it does not, you have not got it right yet.

Now ask yourself: What benefit do I get out of the fulfilment of this vision? What benefit do others get out of it? Correct your vision until it does not contain anything that might harm another. At least find some sort of compromise serving as an optimum solution.

If this is being done as a group action, the many wishes, desires and purposes of all participants must be voiced. Then they must be condensed and formulated as the ideal state, no matter how impossible that dream might sound. The ideal state must be comprehensible, unequivocal, and worded in an attractive way. It must have an emotional touch, and inspire excitement.

Step 2 – the Final Exchangeable Product: What to produce?

What do you need to produce on a regular basis in order to approach the fulfilment of your ideal state? What goals do you need to set for yourself?

What do you need to create or produce to gain the support of others? Of society, of your clients, your neighbours, of anyone involved in your vision? Who will give you goods, money, or support in exchange for what you are going to produce? It is the amount of exchange you are getting which demonstrates the value your product has in the eyes of the world.

Ask yourself: Does this Final Exchangeable Product really get me closer to my vision? And might its production, the selling, or the using of it harm anyone? Adjust it accordingly.

Step 3 – Organisation: How to produce it?

How exactly are you going to produce this Final Exchangeable Product? Brainstorm this. Let all pertinent goals and actions come to mind; note them down.

Now put these goals and actions in order of seniority. Which actions are on the top, and which ones are comprised within the top ones? This way you are creating "action levels".

Now determine details: Who is going to do a specific action? When? Who or what will this depend on? Who or what might get in the way? How are you going to deal with it?

Step 4 – Rules: What to go by?

What conduct needs to be observed to make the game activities smoothly reach their goals?

Make a list of all rules and regulations which already exist within society and are connected with your goals and actions. Create new rules as needed.

Ask yourself with each rule you are creating or applying: Does this really take me closer towards the fulfilment of my vision? Does this rule really facilitate things or does it make them more complicated?

Step 5 – Statistics: Is it going in the right direction?

Which observations might serve to indicate that things are moving in the right direction? Define statistics (exact figures on specific events) and indicators (broadly observed events).

Homework

After you have worked this out as a draft, review it again and again. Be careful to spot contradictions and omissions. Align each step with each other step; make it one whole. Fine-tune it every now and then.

Game over – now what?

Briefly reviewing this chapter, some conclusions can be drawn.

How does one keep a game going? By upholding goals and ideals, and by inspiring hope for their fulfilment in one's players.

How does one destroy a game? By diluting ideals, by distorting them, by discarding them. By not communicating successes or presenting them sarcastically. By spreading bad news. By being a spoilsport purposefully, by taking the joy out of the game.

When is a game over? When its ideal state has been fulfilled. When the dream has become reality. That is the most beautiful outcome.

Far less beautiful it is when the ideal state comes to be recognised as invalid, as out of reach, as unattainable. When obstacles and enemies become too mighty. Then, too, is a game over, but here it is so out of frustration.

Even then the game is only seemingly over. Because in the minds of the players it continues. They pine for the lost dream. For decades, sometimes for generations.

In both cases, in the event of winning as well as losing, there must be a new game! Because without a game, there is no future. And without a future there will be disorientation.

Disorientation leads to quarrels and strife. Eventually, lacking relevant goals and ideals, the players will attack each other and tear each other to bits. No matter whether they have won or lost previously.

When people get disoriented they will turn against each other. This is why you need to create a game for them to play.

3

Organisation

The word "organisation" is derived from a Greek word meaning "tool, implement". Organisation could therefore be said to be the tool or implement for putting ideas into reality.

Organisation can be described as splitting up a complex undertaking into plans, programs and projects. It also means to assign tasks to the players available. "Fred, you do this. Joe, you do that. Sue, this job is for you." And so on.

Put differently, this means: a game leader or manager puts hats on people.

Putting hats on heads

A hat is a symbol of recognition. People with tin hats are soldiers, people with blue hats are airline pilots, people with red and white hats are Santa Clauses. People with tall white hats are cooks. And so on.

The dictionary defines it as follows: The word "hat" signifies an office which is symbolised by a special hat, even when the office holder is not actually wearing that hat. For example, the two principal hats a president or prime minister wears are those of ceremonial head of state and chief executive.

Hats express a function

A hat can be described as a specific task assigned to a person. From people with hats one expects a specific performance. One expects a specific being, doing and having.

Example: A traffic policeman controls the traffic at a cross-roads in order to keep all the cars moving. So who is he being? A policeman. What is he doing? Directing cars. What is his intended product, his result, his having? Traffic moving smoothly. Does he obtain it in actual fact? He does. Good man.

With the stationmaster, the airline pilot, the cook, it is the same story. From a person wearing a hat you would expect specific results. Therefore you would be rather startled to see a person with a fireman's helmet on his head flying your holiday airplane.

A hat services a functional need. When certain particles keep appearing which need to be processed in a prescribed way, a hat will appear all by itself. It contains a being, a doing and a having.

Example: In a family of five, amongst many other things, meals have to be prepared. For that the shopping needs to be done. Before the meal the table needs to be laid; after the meal the dishes need to be washed, and the rubbish taken out.

So in this process of feeding the family certain particles come routinely into play which need to be processed in a prescribed way. In the case of our example five functions need to be fulfilled to serve a meal – five hats need to be worn: the shopper, the cook, the table arranger, the dishwasher, the rubbish cleaner. These labels signify the "being" of each hat. What their "doing" and their "having" has to be is a matter of definition and agreement.

All five hats could be worn by one person always, or by each family member in turn, or by whosoever happens to feel like it that day. That is a matter of agreement. But that they have to be worn is for certain, otherwise the house will look a mess.

The value and challenge of a hat

Life suppresses and enslaves many people; it makes them confused. They believe they are not worth much.

However, when you put hats on them, when you assign specific tasks to them they can fulfil, that gives them an identity. Now they have a clearly defined area of responsibility. Before they were nobody; now they are somebody. (This works beautifully on children!)

Putting hats on people makes them feel safe and confident.

However, along with this new being (expressed by the hat) goes the obligation for a doing and a having. It is not sufficient to hand a hat over to people, thus assigning them a brand new being, without also stating the obligations. "You are going to be the cashier and you the managing director." – "If we win the election, you are going to be the minister of economics and you the minister of finance." – "After the rebellion you are going to get the senior command of the army."

The promise of becoming elevated to unprecedented importance is certainly nice and flattering to the individuals involved. But does it also fall in line with their capabilities? Because in the end what is significant is not the being, not the big name, but the having – the good results.

Is this player willing and able to achieve what the doing and the having of his hat require? Which is to say, is he competent? And given his good intentions, does he have the necessary willingness to go ahead and actually do it?

If so, he is worth his weight in gold. If not, he is adding deadweight to the game. Or worse, he may even lead it off its purpose.

Those in love with the framed certificates hanging on their walls see only the glory of their own being; they are not really co-players. They risk succumbing to the seductiveness of the title and the power assigned to their hat and misusing their new positions.

When people accept hats they should recognise what is expected of them. They should feel confident that they are up to it in terms of competence and willingness. Should they fulfil these requirements, then motivation, activity, and success are programmed.

In a sensibly organised community where everybody knows

and wears their hat, you will find no criminality. That is a historical and ethnological fact. In such a community everybody knows their position, what is demanded of them, and what they can demand of others. They know their rights and duties. Their duties they fulfil; their rights they demand.

Wearing the hats of others

Supporting a troubled player is noble and human. One carries his load until he can walk again. One helps him wear his hat, and even wears it in his stead for a while. However, if that player needs to see himself in the role of "victim of adverse circumstances", or if one loves oneself in the role of the charitable do-gooder, the actual goal of the game will slowly fade into oblivion. Because neither of the two is wearing his or her hat any longer.

Being overly helpful will defeat a game.

At the onset one has set out to produce a certain product. However, should the name of the game become: "How can I help my fellow man?" this in turn becomes too much of a load, and the ship sinks.

How to build a good team

A good manager does not hand posts to his buddies, unless he intends to ruin the game (or have a different game in mind), at which point he is of course not a good manager.

A good manager selects people who are able to wear their hats. People who are able to fill the being assigned to them, with the appropriate doing, and who get the appropriate results. People who have the ability and stamina to pull through the initial bumpy passages until the show runs well. Such players are truly competent.

Competence consists of knowledge, responsibility, and the ability to control.

Knowledge can be acquired from research, books and courses, and from experiences had under good supervision.

Knowledge is not the problem. Responsibility and control however – that is where the difficulty starts.

Take Fred for example. Fred has enormous knowledge but is limited with regard to control. He is able to control routine procedures reliably but scared to make decisions the moment they go beyond the usual framework. He shies away from responsibility. So in the final analysis, Fred is to be considered incompetent within the fullness of his role.

Knowledge combined with low responsibility means in effect low ability to control. And that means incompetence.

Now let us take a look at Sue. Despite having considerable experience she has enormous problems with deadlines. Yes, it always works out, but only just, with huffing and puffing, at the very last minute, and sometimes too late. Her desk is covered with books and papers, her communication baskets flow over, piles and piles of folders on the floor. Every night late hours, and she still does not take anything to a decent conclusion. She has no control over her Performance Packages. Again: incompetence.

To repeat the point: knowledge is not the problem, as it can be acquired easily. But responsibility and control – these are questions of personal character; this is where we get in touch with the psyche and the soul of a person. It is for this reason that it is so hard to enhance responsibility and control.

But most definitely one should strive to do so. A great deal can be achieved by well-focused coaching. There are strategies for in-depth character-building. Anyone willing to learn can be educated.

This works within the given limits of a particular personality, admittedly, but still: Making a good man more competent and valuable has never been wrong. But kicking a good man out has always been wrong – just as wrong as attempting to pamper a hopeless case.

Personality development

Regardless of whether we discuss training, trainers, and trainees; coaches and "coachees"; professors and students – in the end it all comes down to education, to teaching someone something useful. So we might as well use the old-fashioned terms "teacher" and "pupil".

What is the purpose of teaching? Not, one should hope, to enable someone to repeat parrot-fashion, but to make a personality grow to larger dimensions of understanding and competence.

Good education presupposes that pupil and teacher agree on a goal. The pupil must be willing to attain the goal as much as the teacher. The teacher must be willing to pave the way towards the goal; and he must never appear doubtful about his ability to do so.

If the teacher is certain about his teaching ability, if the pupil wishes to attain the goal on his own account, and if the teacher knows that the pupil trusts him, the teacher may rightfully be tough when needed, and he won't lose the trust of his pupil.

The good teacher loves his pupil and demands everything of him. He is tough. He knows no compromises. Only the best can satisfy him.

A good teacher is interested in his pupil, in his subject, in life. He is interested. He does not make himself interesting. He does not make a show of himself.

Good education, well presented, can be grasped with sensuous delight. It is not abstract. It must be comprehensible and applicable. It must have to do with the life reality of the pupil. If not, the pupil will soon feel as lost as a shipwrecked sailor drifting in the fog.

A good teacher clearly recognises the flaws of his pupil as if they were blinking red lights on a control panel. To correct his pupil, the good teacher points out one single light at a time. He asks his pupil to find the source of the trouble and fix it. The teacher never points out more than one flaw. By doing so he would overwhelm his pupil.

He points out only one flaw at a time. In the beginning he does this gently. Later he does it harder, gradually ever harder; until the pupil has toughened up, and finally knows that he has made it. That is a success for both.

Challenges allow people to grow – as long as the challenges are well proportioned.

A good teacher directs his pupil with praise, not punishment. He directs the attention and energy of his pupil towards positive goals (success) instead of negative ones (dangers and disappointments). This way the pupil will keep foremost in mind what needs doing and less what needs avoiding. So his doing is not blocked through anxiety and fear. His energy keeps on flowing.

Production and organisation in the right balance

Quite often there is a conflict between organisation and production, as if the two stand in opposition to each other.

Organisation means training people, establishing procedures and providing materials and machinery. Organising means predicting and providing: a rather modest, yet still important role compared to the thrills of production.

Production means that someone actually creates something. He has something to demonstrate. He competes with others, he boasts, he stands in the front line. Production means fight, victory, praise, recognition.

Furthermore, organisation costs money. Production, however, brings the money in. For this reason the value of good organisers is not always recognised.

This is where the problem lies. Whilst focusing on all the fun you are having whilst producing, you may forget to organise. This way your game will stay small.

Should your game expand one day, and unexpectedly so, you may not be able to meet the suddenly high production targets because of organisational shortcomings. So what do you get? Chaos, stress, nervous breakdowns.

Conversely, if you chose to organise everything perfectly before you got started, you would die of starvation before getting the shovel into the ground for the first time.

Stress-free growth depends on an even balance between production and organisation.

Hats and functions

A man-made organisation can be compared to a living organism – for example a pulsating sea anemone. Steadily and continuously it pumps in sea water, pumps it out, pumps it in, pumps it out. Without a break. Nutritional particles stream in, get processed, stream out: a balanced exchange with the environment. A well-proportioned give and take.

An organism dies when its harmonious exchange with its environment is disturbed. The same is true for organisations.

Communication is the processing of particles in interaction with the environment. The more your communication is tuned to your environment, the more alive and effective you are.

In a human organisation the "particles being pumped in and out" would be objects (such as products, tools, raw materials, writing gadgets, money), documents (letters, invoices, forms, notepads, bank statements), verbal conversations, phone calls, and e-mails. All of that is part of human communication. All these particles need to be processed in a sensible way.

A useful organisational model would show more than just the

existing hierarchy. It would be more than just a graphical representation of the company structure. Above all, it would clarify functions and the relationship between functions. It would show what is being done, who is doing it, and the expected result.

We are not referring to specific individuals; we are not talking about Joe, Fred or Susan. We are talking about *functions*. This is the same as saying we are talking about hats. Hats are functions.

When Fred leaves the game, another will need to do his job, fulfil his function, wear his hat. The person goes; the hat stays. Someone else will have to wear it, because with no-one supporting that particular function the game will break down.

A useful organisational model would show the being, doing and having of the game to which it refers. In particular it would describe the interaction of hats. It would specifically describe which communication particles are supposed to flow from one hat to the next, and how they are to be processed by each hat before being passed to the next hat.

To ensure that this happens is the function of management.

Management ensures the being, doing, and having of a game as prescribed by its Game Concept, and as defined by its organisational model.

The idea or vision a game begins with is its mental or spiritual character. This is its core, its *being*.

The co-ordination of the communication particles flowing in and out of the game in exchange with the environment; the alignment of activities with respect to a desired result; the assignment of actions to hats – that is the *doing* of a game.

What is being produced by the game, the Final Exchangeable Product, be it livestock, plants, machines, or services – that is the *having* of a game.

47

An all-purpose Organisational Model

In the terminology of contemporary business academies, management is usually described in terms of "processes" and "work flows". This is certainly useful for large companies, but for a self-employed person who is a one-man show, or for a small business with half a dozen employees, it can be much too theoretical.

For practical purposes it is much easier to look at any activity, whether large or small, as comprising nine senior functions, as this chapter describes. Such an Organisational Model consisting of nine senior hats will be referred to as an Org Model for short.

It will become evident that all of these nine hats need to be worn. They form a whole, or perhaps are aspects of a whole. It follows that the efficiency and success of a game will decrease through weaknesses in, or non-existence of, one or the other of these nine hats.

Should you wish to do an analysis of your own or any other business, you could use this Org Model as a framework. Take a particular weakness of the game in question, and then find out which of those nine hats is not worn correctly.

Before the start: the Founder

A game, as we know, always starts with an idea. Somebody has an idea, wishes to realise it, works out a Game Concept, and consequently becomes the founder of a game.

The actual product of a game founder is "a well-worked out Game Concept".

The founder is no hat within the game. Being the creator of the game, he stands above and outside it.

Should the founder take it upon himself to actually run the game, he will be inside the game. If in the beginning stages of the game he is the one and only player, he will have to wear all nine hats. There is no-one else to do it!

As the game grows and draws in some players, the nine hats

can gradually be delegated to others. However, regardless of the number of players joining together on this playing field, nine hats will need to be worn to make it happen successfully.

Hat 1: President

The President represents the spirit of the game internally and externally, i.e. to the players as well as to the public. His main role is to ensure that its Game Concept is adhered to. When he achieves this convincingly, he has "ethical presence", and for that he is respected.

Hat 2: Legal Advisor

Someone has to make sure that the game is played in a legally safe environment, and wear the hat of Legal Advisor. This could be an outside professional. He doesn't have to be "part of the company". He is called when needed. This ensures that this hat is worn.

Hat 3: Director/Chief Executive

The Executive Director, or perhaps General Manager, monitors the totality of all the procedures within the game.

He is right at the pulse of what is happening. He is associated with all game players either directly or indirectly. He evaluates and interprets statistics and indicators, analyses the existing scene, and plans the steps necessary to take the game closer to its ideal state. He directs, monitors and corrects activities within the organisation.

Hat 4: Establishment

Establishment concerns itself with organising all prerequisites for production. It recruits personnel, ensures the existence and efficiency of internal and external communication systems such as telephones, computers, and mail delivery, and it has routinely needed materials at the ready, for example pen, paper, stationery, tools, company cars, etc.

Hat 5: Customer Liaison (or Marketing)

Here the market is studied to reach potential clients. Is the game with its products and services really needed? Who needs it? How can I reach them? How can it be improved to be more in demand? Customer Liaison also retains contact with existing customers and clients, and monitors customer satisfaction.

Hat 6: Finance Controller

The finance controller is responsible for all financial issues of the organisation: sales, purchases, assets, reserves, cash flows and budgets. The iron rule of the Controller: "Make more than you spend."

Hat 7: Production

Whatever the product or service of this game, whatever its Final Exchangeable Product, these are the people manufacturing it.

Hat 8: Quality Control

Is the Final Exchangeable Product up to standard? Does the game as such, with all its procedures, correspond to the ideal state laid down in the Game Concept? Is the team happy? This is the concern of Quality Control.

Hat 9: Public Relations

When Quality Control has found the Final Exchangeable Product faultless it may now rightfully be promoted to the world, and this is the role of Public Relations. They pour the name of the company through all available media to firmly anchor it on the market.

The secret is in the hologram

These nine hats can be found in all sorts of variations and titles in any human activity, company, or game. Not only in business – anywhere!

Each of the nine "senior hats" can of course be split up into any number of "junior hats".

There is a certain logic to the hats being nine in number. It reflects the underlying organisational principle of be-do-have.

The *being* of the game, its spirit, is represented by the President, the Legal Advisor, and the General Manager.

The *doing* of the game, its energy aspect, is carried forth by Establishment, Customer Liaison, and Finance Controlling. Communication lines inside the game, as well as with customers, means energy, likewise the money flow.

The *having* of the game is realised not only by the actual Production but also by Quality Control and Public Relations, since with no product there, what would they have to do?

It should now have become apparent that the triad "be-do-have" applies to any organisational dimension, large or small. One discovers it from top to bottom, from the overall game as the largest dimension, down to each individual hat. With this, it can rightfully be deemed an infinite organisational principle, a "fractal".

Be-do-have is the basic building block which repeats itself on all levels high and low. That is the meaning of the word "fractal". If, for simplicity's sake, you took a brick to be a constructional fractal in architecture, then the whole building would have to look like a brick, and each room would have to resonate with the dimensions of the brick.

In reality things are somewhat more complex, be it in architecture or in nature, but this example may demonstrate the concept: that a fractal is a basic building block the dimensions of which are to be found on all levels of a given piece of architecture, music, philosophy, landscape form, or of an organism.

In a highly coherent game the Game Concept would be fractally reflected on each and every level. All players, all decisions, all actions would correspond to the Game Concept. It would be felt wherever you went and with whomever you spoke.

This also occurs when a hologram is broken: each fragment contains the complete image.

Contributions always welcome!

If players on lower management ranks ("juniors") were to think for themselves, then players on higher management ranks ("seniors") would not need to think for their juniors – would that not save an enormous amount of time and energy? Most certainly.

If juniors, eager to act to solve a burning problem, did not have to sit and wait for a senior to at long last come to an end of his thinking – would that not save even more time? It would.

You want to get people to think and take on responsibility? You would like to encourage them to participate and contribute? You would prefer to see a higher emotional tone in your company, showing up as less frustration and fewer sick leaves? There is a simple recipe:

Use Decision Proposals as a form of organisational communication!

How to work out a Decision Proposal

1. The situation: In only a few words briefly sketch the situation to be resolved. ("I cannot pick Pablo up from the airport.")

2. The context (how this is a problem): Now add all relevant information so as to convey the full picture of the situation, its complexity and its context. ("My car broke down. Pablo has no mobile phone. He is due to arrive at the airport in an hour, and he will get lost as he doesn't speak English.")

This explanation should be said in a few lines. If any more space is needed one should attach a separate documentation, be it a single sheet or a thousand pages. The actual Decision Proposal should be brief. The person to whom it is addressed should be able to take it in at one glance.

3. Suggested solution: The writer of the Decision Proposal suggests a solution. It is arrived at plausibly and comprehensibly on the basis of the data given. ("With your agreement, could I use your car to pick him up?")

The player formulating the Decision Proposal is called upon to think of a solution himself. That is the whole trick. The junior does not pass the problem to the boss. He works it out himself.

Why? Because he should know the job at hand and the whole area better than anyone else. Because he may already know a solution nobody else would have considered. Because working out a solution increases his decision-making skills, happiness and responsibility – and so his competence.

Organisational communication lines

A Decision Proposal is usually sent "upwards", i.e. to the next management level. This is because in a game you will naturally find two directions of communication: the vertical and the horizontal. "Upwards" and "across".

On horizontal lines, i.e. on the same management level, you get routine communication regarding ongoing activities. In soccer this would be the team members playing the ball to each other.

The vertical line becomes important in non-ordinary situations. One would send a Decision Proposal upwards and receive the necessary approval or order from above. In soccer this would mean asking the team captain or the trainer to step in.

On the vertical line a Decision Proposal would take the following route: It goes upwards to the senior player to whom it is addressed. It is either approved or rejected, and then sent back down.

If approved, it is immediately turned into an order. If disapproved, a good reason is given. A *good* reason, in writing! Not a brush-off.

So in brief: horizontally, it is routine communication. Vertically, it is Decision Proposal going upwards, and orders running downwards.

Secrecy is an explosive

When a Decision Proposal on its way up runs through a number of hats, no decision maker along the line should be bypassed. Everybody involved in the matter should be put on the routing, permitted to look at the issue, and if needed comment upon it. No secrecy! Secrecy creates tensions. Secrecy is a powder keg which can blow up the whole place.

The same is true for reports regarding non-optimum situations, and in particular complaints. Whenever possible, play the game openly, not behind other people's back. Better to handle it with no secrecy.

For example, when a player does not get along well with another, and the usual conversations do not lead to a resolution, the affected person should have the possibility to put a complaint in at the department of personnel (Hat 7, Quality Control).

In order to prevent a whispering campaign against the accused, the complaint should be put in writing. The people involved should get together with a mediator, and talk it through. Each person mentioned in the complaint should be handed a copy of it, also the accused of course.

This may lead to considerable flare-ups within the group. But it is better to have one decent flare-up of short duration than year-long intrigues, suspicions, and mobbing campaigns. Usually conflicts between personnel are resolved with only essential details exposed until the matter is settled. This may not be sufficient, though.

Secrecy is an explosive which can tear a team to bits. It can make a whole game go up in smoke.

Provided a game is played in the spirit of self-determinism, the players have the right to be correctly informed on the state of the game. One should not withhold such data from one's players.

As a final note on secrecy: not all secrecy is harmful. For example, you wouldn't give a surprise away – think of Christmas presents and birthday gifts. Neither would you tell someone who is very ill that his dog just got run over by a car.

So there certainly is benevolent secrecy, yes. It means well. The explosive type of secrecy is malevolent; it is ill-intentioned

Captain and crew

To use a comparison, game leader and players can be likened to a captain and his crew. The crew members are on deck or below deck and look after their various jobs. They do not see much of the high seas but are very aware of the internal state of the ship.

The captain, however, sits up on the bridge. He overviews the sea, the stormy waves, the hostile reefs and the evil pirates. Of the state of the ship he only knows what his crew tells him. So in order to take the ship safely to port the captain must know all data: the external ones from the environment (his own observations), and also the internal ones from the inside of the ship (the observations of the crew).

Captain and crew depend on each other. For this reason the captain cannot simply do as he likes; neither can he follow each and every suggestion of the crew. He has more data at his fingertips than anyone else aboard ship. To make wise decisions he must consider the totality of the data at hand. And he must be able to give good reasons for his decisions on the basis of these data.

When you see someone refusing to give good reasons for his decisions, you can bet there is an arbitrary factor in the game.

And that means there is also some secrecy.

When the reasoning behind executive decisions is false or pretentious, this is tantamount to patronising the players. Arbitrariness and privilege-mindedness have won the day.

Occasionally however – and specifically when there is danger afoot and immediate action is required – the captain will have to act "above the heads" of his crew. He will have to play out his authority and even become dictatorial for a certain time span. However, he is well advised to take the next opportunity and fill his crew in on what really happened and why.

The captain must keep "decision transparency". That's his obligation towards the crew. If he does not do that, the crew feel they are being disregarded.

An executive making fools of his players will soon find himself in a foolish game: No players left, only pieces.

Organisational illnesses

Team members who need to ask their seniors before they can make decisions feel uncertain in their role. In order to feel sure about themselves they need to ask questions all the time, which may actually block the existing communication lines. Team members who bother their colleagues with routine decisions steal their time.

All these are signs of incompetence. Organisational illness is the consequence.

A player who cannot make sensible decisions within the context of his hat does in fact not wear his hat.

For a game to be played properly one must rely on everybody knowing and wearing their hat, no matter where they stand in the game: up at the top or down below.

There are really only two symptoms of organisational illness: One, hats not known. Two, hats not worn.

Assuming that you as a player noticed that another was not wearing his hat properly, you would not just put his hat on your own head. Particularly not if this leads to overwork, endangering your own hat.

To wear other people's hats "just like that" easily leads to incomplete actions overall, and eventually everybody feels overwhelmed and becomes increasingly stressed.

When you wear the hat of another at all, it should be only as an exception. In an emergency, for example, fast action is required; alternatively if the player in that area is new and fumbling, or hurt, or simply not present, you would naturally step in.

This is practical, but it does imply that you are bypassing your colleague. It is as if he was not there at all, whether physically present or not.

However, if it is so easy to bypass him – is he then perhaps incompetent? Is he superfluous in his post? Is he needed at all? Obviously a person who is regularly bypassed is on track to losing his hat, his job, his position, his income.

When you are being bypassed by a "friendly colleague", your job is in danger.

The player in question must be told loud and clear, after the emergency is over, that one has bypassed him. As an act of respect and politeness one would have to tell him that one has worn his hat temporarily, and hand his hat officially back to him.

However, should this happen too often, it is worrisome. This player obviously needs correcting. One should report it to whoever is in charge of looking after the personnel enhancement.

Illness no. 1: No Boss at Home

On horizontal communication lines nobody should wear the hats of others if it can be helped. However, on the vertical line this is almost unavoidable.

To wear the hats of non-existent juniors is the daily bread of a senior because, when he has no-one to whom to delegate, he has to do the work himself.

Our Org Model comprises nine senior hats, and all of them want wearing! If need be, on a single head.

One can only admire executives who manage to wear the hats of non-existent juniors in addition to their own hat. Usually, however, a senior who is kept busy with the hats of his juniors no longer wears the senior hat (his own).

The consequence: no senior at his post. No boss at home.

Illness no. 2: The Single Ruler

On the other extreme you find the compulsively suspicious senior who would attempt to wear all the hats below him – even though there may be plenty of players to whom to delegate!

This sort of leader does not trust anyone one inch. He cannot grant anyone their own hat. Nobody gets past him. He plays the single ruler.

He is the cork in the neck of the bottle. Because of him there is no flow.

Illness no. 3: The Endless Back and Forth

There is a very common illness that one might call "the endless back and forth". Its symptoms: overheated communication with little result.

Outwardly this is usually presented as "intensive dialogue", "in-depth debate" or "critical discussion". But that is just painting it pink. When communication does not result in practical results, it is a waste of time.

A simple example: Mother and daughter sit at the dinner

table. Says Mother: "Susan, please do not stir your chocolate drink with a knife!" – Daughter: "But Karen's doing it too!" – Mother: "I don't believe this! Next time when I meet her mother I'll ask her. She'd never allow such a thing." – Daughter: "Well, they're on holiday. You can't ask her." – Mother: "Oh really? Where did they go?"

And so on. Mother's original order is forgotten. Susan still stirs her chocolate with a knife. But both are busily "communicating".

A leading executive engaging in an endless back-and-forth initiates the collapse of his own authority. There is no better way.

Executives who can be led up the garden path will not be taken seriously. The only cure for an endless back-and-forth is the relentlessly repeated question: "Where is your product? When can I expect to get it? When exactly?"

This will lead to remarkable explosions on the part of the back-and-forth artist.

Illness no. 4: Fake Work

"Fake work" stands for artificially created work. As that sort of work is not productive it is not real and, therefore, fake. Time and work power are invested without any product. It is work done outside, and with no relation to, the Game Concept. Therefore it is "off". It is not on the line of that game's purpose but off it.

All types of fake work have a common appearance: the players are busy in "tremendously important" activities or projects; they have not a free moment, and suffer from overwork and stress. The sick leave rate goes up. And the statistics fall, fall, fall.

Reason: people are not wearing their hats. Some players perhaps do not even know their hat. Yet when no defined hats exist, the being, doing and having of the game is not known or is misunderstood.

THE FUTURE IS YOURS!

Here is a brief diagnostic quiz for the detection of fake work: "What's your post in this organisation, please?" The answer may be: "I'm the receptionist and typist." Immediate follow-up: "And your product please?" Pause. Then: "Well – um – I – I'm here five days part-time, and I sort of do the stuff that seems to be on then." – "And how satisfied are you with your job?" – "Well, actually, the stress in this place just wears me out. In two weeks I'm going to be off on sick leave to have some treatment in a sanatorium."

Instead of her saying: "My product? Excellently typed business letters, cheerfully received telephone calls, efficiently answered e-mails."

But no, she does not know her product; she does everything except wear her own hat. Everybody can come round and give her a job to do, so she wears everybody else's hats halfway, and none of them properly. She makes herself everybody's maidservant. Always too much to do, stress. "Solution": she goes to get some treatment in a sanatorium.

Fake work, without a shadow of doubt.

The art of delegating work

To delegate work you hand your hat over, in full or in part.

When leaving your post you would be well advised – in the name of the game! – to hand your hat over to your successor.

Should you receive a new player on your part of the playing field, you would, in order to free yourself up, happily delegate parts of your job to him.

In order to hand your hat over it is always advisable to write it down. With small hats it can be done verbally of course. Either way, one teaches the new person how to do it correctly.

Unless you are fully in the clear on the being, doing and having of your hat, you will not be able to delegate it reliably. To do so you will have to work out a full Game Concept for your hat. Not an easy task at all! But it is worth it. For how is one supposed to delegate jobs to people when the complexity of one's own post is not clear even to oneself?

You can only teach someone something when you are not immersed totally inside that particular area. In order to pass your hat on to another you must by necessity stand above your own area with ease and grace; you really ought to be a master.

Writing down one's personal Game Concept forces one to clarify to oneself all of one's routine acting and thinking patterns. In writing it down, one puts one's knowledge out in the open. This is the only way to delegate.

Without a fully worked-out Game Concept, in writing, for a given game area, the successful delegation of tasks to juniors, colleagues, or successors is not possible.

4

Synergetic Leadership

To understand and practise synergetic leadership one has to have a concept of synergy. Synergy means: two energies working *with* each other instead of against each other. In nature this is seen in the vortex of a tornado. In sports this is seen in the spiral motions of Judo and particularly Aikido.

As can be shown by these examples, synergetic action builds up a strong flow containing enormous power. Opposition, in contrast, builds walls, dams, and ridges. Mountain ridges are the result of opposing forces; so are standing waves. There is no flow, and all the inherent power results in a standstill.

From the example of eastern martial arts it can well be seen that synergy does not only come into play when the two energies in question are well-meaning. Even an opposing energy with hostile intent can be controlled if the principles of synergy are applied.

For a leader to operate with synergy he would have to understand motivation. To understand motivation he would have to understand emotion. And to understand emotion he would have to feel comfortable with communication. This is the subject of this chapter.

Seven virtues in communication

Successful communication consists of no more than seven factors or perhaps virtues: find your centre – tune in – keep your poise – have firm intention – respect your partner – persist down to the end – be compassionate.

These are virtues one can practise. Day by day! And improve. Let us look at them in detail.

First virtue: Find your centre, be calm

Being centred means you have your head free; you feel quiet and still inside. Thus you are set up to have full attention on the outside world.

When a million things whirl through your head, you cannot pay attention either to your communication partner or to the subject or your environment. Your attention is tied up. With many thought fragments shooting through your head you have no free attention at your disposal; you will appear dispersed. Things may pass you without noticing and you may talk oddly and in a confused way. However, when you are centred you have the power to focus and direct attention.

How to get there? Meditation (or mindfulness): Close your eyes, watch your breathing, focus on your belly button. Wait till the mind calms down.

Have no illusion about this: it may take years of training. Meditation is mind training, simple as that.

Second virtue: Tune in

Attention is the copper cable between communication partners. Through this cable emotional energies and telepathic information can flow. In order to reach your partner, you must tune in to him or her. Do not barge in noisily to unload whatever is on your mind and then disengage. Nobody will have been with you. How would they? Because *it is up to you* to be with them!

Tune in to the spirit of the moment. The prerequisite of course is your own calm. Find and hold the attention of communication partners; get on their emotional wavelength. Words and sentences spoken without attention and "out of tune" appear like mere noises. They do not reach one's communication partner. He may hear them with his ears, but not catch them in his mind.

Third virtue: Keep your poise

Whatever you are perceiving, in particular differing opinions or opinions about you as a person, you should be able to accept it without reacting, breaking down, or falling to bits. Without budging or giving in, you should be able to allow your communication partner his outpourings.

Leave him as he is. It should not bother you. You remain calm, centred and tuned in with him. Stay with him, and let your calmness do its work. A genuinely friendly and interested attitude will always win. Rage, anger and fear will not.

Fourth virtue: Have firm intention

Intention is a force. It puts power behind a message. Without your firm intention your message will not reach the receiver. Putting a handful of "attention flakes" onto the receiver is not sufficient to create and maintain your communication line. In order to get something across through this cable, you need a large amount of those attention flakes; you need to focus them; you need to give them an extra push. That is what we mean by willpower.

Intention pushes a message from sender to receiver. Intention is the determination for a message to really reach there. When this is lacking, the message will hang up halfway or dissipate.

Fifth virtue: Be respectful

Pay attention to how your communication partner feels. Put yourself in his shoes and consider his viewpoint. Acknowledge him for what you perceive of him. Such an acknowledgement means that you have noticed him and value him. He will positively respond to such signs of recognition and respect.

For example: Somebody has asked a question, given an order, or simply voiced an opinion – he has communicated something. Now he is in a state of tension. He expects a signal from the receiver, a signal of understanding, for example: "Yes, I got this." Or: "The answer to your question is so-and-so." Or: "Your order will be executed at such-and-such a time!"

Without any acknowledgement the sender will come to believe that there is nobody at the other end of the communication line. He will feel like he was talking to a wall. His tenseness remains. Very frustrating, very demotivating.

However, the moment the sender is acknowledged by the receiver for what he said (content), for how he said it (emotion), and for what he intended to communicate (significance), the sender can respond. Finally someone has understood what he always wanted to say! No further words are necessary. End of communication.

Through a word or gesture you have let him know: "Yes, I have noted what you're doing, saying, and feeling." With that you are actually telling him: "I have noticed *you*."

This does not necessarily imply agreement! Acknowledging is not the same as agreeing. You can still reserve an opinion of your own, but this may not be the point in time to voice it.

By acknowledging adequately, you are actually creating the players of your game. Getting acknowledged motivates tremendously. It makes a huge difference.

Only when a player feels properly acknowledged will he wish to continue the game. Regardless of whether he is commended for his good achievements, acknowledged for routine production, or reprimanded for his mistakes – the decisive factor is: you have noticed him! And so he will get on with the job or even do better.

Proper acknowledgement is the secret of leadership.

Sixth virtue: Persist

Excellent results do not appear spontaneously. You as a leader cannot just give one instruction and then leave your players alone with the game. It takes persistence and empathy to keep them moving towards the ideal state of the game. Persistence and empathy are the final two virtues on our catalogue of seven.

Situation: You have demanded something specific, but you

did not get what you wanted. Instead you got something similar, something different, something temporary. You are not satisfied.

In order to get what you really wanted, you will have to uphold your intention, no matter for how long. Instead of engaging in unnecessary discussions, you would simply repeat your question or order politely, and insist on the exact answer, on the exact compliance. That's persistence.

No rage, no anger! Instead you would stay centred, tuned in, stable, determined and respectful. And when you eventually get the answer to your question or the execution of your command, immediately acknowledge it!

The acknowledgement marks the end of this specific Performance Package. Its beginning was the order given or the question asked. You are now free to start the next Performance Package.

Seventh virtue: Have empathy

When persistence alone does not get you there, when emotions are welling up, you need to be compassionate. You need to have empathy.

When fellow players have built up emotional barriers (anger, frustration, fear, sadness, resignation), when physical pains are in the way – that's when compassion is required. If you merely repeated your questions or commands, you would make things worse.

Example: You may tell a typist ten times that a half a dozen important letters must be typed soonest – yet when she is in love or has a toothache she will not listen. You may repeat this twenty times: with no effect. She might even get upset. When all you did was repeat a request at work! So what went wrong? Answer: you did not tune in sufficiently to her condition. Therefore you did not show any compassion.

Compassion means to understand and acknowledge one's fellow players from *their* viewpoint, and to encourage them.

Truly understanding and honestly encouraging is the essence of motivation.

In the example above: "Yes, I do understand that you're dreaming of your new boyfriend. You do like him, don't you?" – Now you see her coming out of her dreams; she looks at you; she notices you. The moment you have her attention, you can follow it up with: "Could you perhaps still get these letters typed before the end of the day?" – And yes, she will. Because you have reached her.

Smooth communication cycles are the prerequisite for smooth production cycles.

The logic of emotions

Human communications are carried forward by emotions. Emotions cannot be removed from human communication. Impossible.

Each perception of one's environment is an act of communication. Seeing, hearing, smelling, touching, tasting are acts of communication. And each of those sensory perceptions is coupled with emotions, with pleasure or disgust, with like or dislike.

Anything that lives and feels generates emotional impulses and reacts to them. "Emotion", derived from the Latin root *ex movere*, means: "something that moves or flows from the inside outward".

Examples of emotional levels are: joy, interest, benevolence, contentment, boredom, rage, anger, fear, sadness, apathy. In this sequence. Emotions follow a downward motion, level by level. With each new frustration you sink deeper.

"Well, that looks pretty, doesn't it?" could be said in a dozen different ways: each time on a different level of emotion.

Emotions can be likened to a pair of coloured glasses. Through them one perceives one's environment. An angry person sees red. To those in love, everything is pink. To someone who just suffered a loss or a breakdown, the world is black.

One never sees one's environment as it really is. One sees it as one feels: through the filter of one's emotions. And one acts accordingly.

Players have emotions. No game runs without emotions. If you as a leader wish to really understand your fellow players, you must consider not only the factual content of their communication but also the emotional element within.

Communication is not restricted to verbal dialogue. When you give your girlfriend a bunch of roses or a diamond necklace, that is definitely a communication, and you would hope for her to understand its significance. Throwing bombs also is a form of communication.

The difference is in the *medium*: language, roses, bombs. In either case we are dealing with a factual, an emotional, and an intentional aspect. What the sender wishes to communicate is one thing; how he packages his communication quite another.

Computer networks, telephones, satellite television and similar gadgets make worldwide communication possible. But at the two ends of these instruments sit quite ordinary people: people with emotions.

In the final analysis, despite all the technology transporting their communication, the senders and receivers of communication are human beings. Technology may do a beautiful job as a communication *medium*, but it cannot replace human beings as instigators and evaluators of communication.

Frustration: downward step by step

As described above, no player lives without emotions; no game runs without emotions. Emotions are tied in with frustration. Just as there are levels of emotion there are also levels of frustration. The two go hand in hand.

In high spirits you feel certain of your victory. In a bad mood you see only barriers. Should those barriers prove to be insurmountable, you will feel frustrated.

Frustration is taken from the Latin word *frustra*, which means "in vain". Frustration therefore means: "experiencing the pointlessness of one's efforts". Frustrated people no longer wish to play. They are demotivated. They lack drive.

Frustration builds up gradually. It is not either "totally frustrated" or "not frustrated at all". No, it is a gradual descent, step by step, down towards the dark basement of apathy.

In brief: the scale begins at the top with victoriousness, goes through eagerness and effort, and takes you down to inhibition, resignation, and refusal.

The scale of frustration

Victoriousness. In the beginning of a game the players feel *victorious* and enthusiastic. They have a goal and are dead certain that they will achieve it.

Eagerness. As soon as the first obstacles come in, the enthusiasm tends to cool off a little. What remains is *eagerness* in the expectation of the successes soon to be experienced.

Effort. Eagerness takes one happily along for a while. Yet again one runs into obstacles! Success does not seem to come by itself. Now one is attempting to force it. Go, go, go! Hard labour and *effort*. Clenched fists, gritted teeth, rage, anger.

Inhibition. When the obstacles prove to be insurmountable, disappointment sets in. It shows itself as an *inhibition* to carry on. One feels weighed down and depressed. It becomes hard to even move. Another few setbacks and one drops down into *resignation*.

Resignation. Now, as one is moving on half steam anyway, one will no longer make much headway. One begins to see the whole enterprise as pointless. The goal appears unreachable.

Refusal. At the bottom end, one step further down, one is no longer willing to be in touch with one's former game. One denies ever having been part of it, and calls those mad who are still with it. An utter *refusal* of the originally cherished vision has set in. To do an about-turn against the game which previously one has championed – that is the deepest level of frustration.

The enemy within

With each new, insurmountable obstacle, there is the danger of going one step further down the scale. Each of these steps may be a platform for life and continue on for years. For decades! Why? Because one now believes that one cannot make it. One has accepted that the external resistance is insurmountable.

With this, one has pulled the external resistance inward to oneself. One has turned it into internal resistance. The internal resistance is the worse of the two. It prevents one from pursuing one's path further.

Only the limits which we set for ourselves can stop us for real.

How do you pull a fellow player out of his frustration? How do you motivate him? This is the subject of the next section.

Understanding on three levels

Understanding is a highly complex affair. Firstly you would have to pick up what your partner has actually said; you would have to get the factual content of his message. Then you have to get his emotions. And then, what his statement is meant to signify. Three levels of understanding!

"Gee, look at the plants," says Linda to Joe. "Hasn't it been rather dry lately? I wonder if that garden hose is still intact."

Joe got all that, except the last part. "What do you mean by 'garden nose'?" he asks.

"I said 'hose'," answers Linda. "And I actually mean 'hose'. I do not mean 'nose', 'rose' or 'pose'."

"Oh, hose. I see." Joe has now grasped the content of the incoming message, the actual words. Now follows the next part: Joe has to mentally put those words into the right category, in the right mental drawer.

"Hose" is what Linda has said. Now what is a hose? Does she mean those pink things wriggling about in the garden? No, those are worms. Ah, then it has to be one of those long slithery creatures with no legs. No, those are snakes. Well, perhaps it is that flexible type of plastic tubing you use for watering the garden? Right, that must be it. That is what a hose is.

First Joe has mentally photocopied the content of the message. Then he has compared it with what he already knows, and eventually has put it in the right mental drawer – and with that he has finally understood. At least in terms of its reality content.

Moving on: if Joe now cheerfully said to Linda: "I see... It's hoses you're talking about!", Linda would consider him an idiot. Even though Joe got the content right!

Content therefore is not all there is to a message, not all by far. There is also the aspect of emotion; and furthermore, the aspect of intended significance.

Did Joe detect a note of concern in Linda's voice? She certainly didn't sound cheerful when she commented on the state of her plants. So Joe says: "Something worrying you, dear?" And Linda barks back at him with: "Of course there is!"

Although Joe got Linda's emotion right, this did not exactly create happiness. What did Joe do wrong? What's amiss?

Well, he did not pick up her intention. What is it that Linda actually meant to say? What do her words signify? The real message is found on a level way above content and emotion. The real message lies in the significance of Linda's words.

Joe has a bright moment. "Guess I had better get busy and water the garden," he says. "Now you're talking!" says Linda. And they lived happily ever after.

The "Three Levels of Understanding"

Reality: *What* was said?

Emotion: *How* was it said?

Significance: What was *meant?*

Only when the receiver of the message has comprehended the message on all three levels will the sender feel fully understood.

Equally the sender also has a responsibility. It is to tailor his message in terms of content and emotion to the level of reality and emotion of the receiver. It is a matter of being aware of context and circumstances, a matter of tuning in. When the sender does not do this, his message will not get there.

The art of motivation

The art of motivation consists of three steps: firstly, under-standing; secondly, acknowledging with empathy; thirdly, leading back to the subject or job which was deviated from.

Step 1: Understand. Understand the factual and emotional situation of your fellow player; get the significance that his situation has for him. See it from *his* viewpoint.

Step 2: Acknowledge. Acknowledge your fellow player with the necessary empathy. Get it across to him that you see his situation and understand it fully. Part of the acknowledgement is practical: look after his needs and troubles and help him through, emotionally as well as pragmatically. This may take time. No sweet talk will do! You have to really mean it.

Step 3: Lead back. Tactfully remind your fellow player of the game and the ideals you share. Gently rebuild his willingness to be with it and play along.

A leader wishing to motivate his fellow players must master these three steps, bearing in mind the seven communication virtues outlined above.

Rewards and acknowledgements

The reward, the bonus, the medal – they each serve as rather solid, tangible forms of acknowledgement. A good leader would never forget to reward good achievements. This is because a player who is fully motivated within the game considers his products vitally important. He gets paid for attaining them and for attaining them in high quality. With his sub-products each player contributes to the attainment of the Final Exchangeable Product. He should be rewarded in proportion to his contributions.

When you judge the achievements of a fellow player on the basis of his products and statistics, he will know that he is being recognised. He will feel personally acknowledged. But when you pay him for the number of hours he has worked, no matter what was done or how well it was done, you demotivate him.

One should permit one's fellow players to participate in the value they are creating. The value of machines can be looked at in terms of cost efficiency and what they produce per hour. However, the value of people is a different matter. Their value lies in their ability to act intelligently and contribute to the furthering of the game. This is precisely what needs to be acknowledged. This is what makes people love and respect a leader.

What is motivating you?

Why does anyone play a game at all? What motivates his zeal? What moves him on? (The words "motive" and "motivate" are derived from the Latin root *movere* meaning "to move". You also find it in words like "motor" and "movement".)

In the business world, motivation is often explained with reference to the "Maslow Pyramid". The psychologist Maslow saw a hierarchy of seven needs, starting at the bottom with the need for food, water, and safety, and ending at the top with the desire for art, beauty, and self-actualization. The idea is that a hungry person won't think much about art and self-actualization. This assumption is of course debatable as one could find many examples where the opposite is true. There were innumerable painters who created masterpieces whilst being half-starved.

One could also look at motivation from the viewpoint of impulses rather than needs as addressed below. Three classes of motives become apparent.

Three classes of motives

Greed. The greedy person does anything for money and personal gain. Free courses, free travel tickets, price-reduced materials, valuable connections. The more of it, the better. He is more interested in getting than in giving.

Conviction. Conviction is always linked with some sort of ideology, some political creed or religious dogma. Someone operating on this motivation likes to justify his participation in a game with many arguments. To him, the satisfaction of being right, of seeing his ideology win, counts more than money or personal gain. "God is on our side" – that is enough for him; that is all he wants to know.

Duty-boundness. The duty-bound player does not pay

THE FUTURE IS YOURS!

particular attention to the question of exchange, at least not in the material sense. He has understood the game, appreciates its value, and gives it his full support. Any given situation he looks over in terms of the whole game context, and decides accordingly. He decides in the name of the game; he decides in terms of goals and visions. When the game goes well, he feels richly recompensed, even though his income happens to be low.

Motives and ethics

From the viewpoint of a leader it is of course best to have many duty-bound players in the game. They are not as costly to retain as the greedy; they are thankful and will not leave the game the moment it no longer pays. Neither do they waste their time preaching or discussing the game like the conviction fanatics do.

Yet, much as the duty-bound player appears to act on a more noble motive than the other two, the consequences of his actions may not be so noble. Because, what consequences a game may have on other games, on innocent bystanders, on the environment, is not easily seen. How the game could be evaluated from a higher viewpoint, from an external point of judgement, is beyond many players, even the duty-bound ones.

Not many people manage to look over the fence of their own game. They are too busy inside the fence. Yet in order to act ethically, one would need to be able to do precisely that: look over the fence of one's own game, and see what it is like on the other side. And then begin to wonder about how one's own game might affect others. (See further the chapter on ethics.)

Praise and blame

A game, if constructed correctly, must have a Game Concept, and ideally all players must know, understand, and agree with it. This makes it possible to judge the qualities of individual players. Those who contribute to the game would be rightfully promoted; those inhibiting it would, equally rightfully, be disciplined.

To put it simply: industriousness should be praised, sloth discouraged. A well set-up game can be recognised by the statistics: tendency upwards or downwards? That forms the basis of judgement.

Four harsh rules

Honouring productiveness furthers productiveness.
Condoning unproductiveness furthers unproductiveness.
Punishing productiveness encourages unproductiveness.
Criticising unproductiveness encourages productiveness.

Choose the game, not the player

Life is frequently brutal, hits one hard, makes one a loser. Losers are naturally frustrated and depressed.

Depressive people are not active. They demand to be carried. They do not lend strength; they weaken. They suck away the strength of stronger individuals.

The stronger ones, from compassion, feel called upon to help those in trouble. But when you carry too many losers on your shoulders, you will soon break down yourself.

Equally, carrying a loser on one's shoulders for too long may make him forget to walk by himself. By being pitied he will not learn to support himself.

So do not pity a loser – that doesn't help at all. Understand him; be compassionate. Motivate him. Return him to the game. But don't wreck the whole game by carrying too many losers on your shoulders for too long.

Group decisions made easy

One huge problem in leadership is how to reach the people one is leading. What do they really think and feel? How can one tell them what to do and meet their agreement rather than their opposition? How to bridge the gap between the top end of management and the bottom level?

Equally, how can a group confront its leaders, and speak for itself? Groups usually make decisions by majority vote. This can leave a minority gritting their teeth and swearing revenge – in particular when the minority feels that their point of view was never duly considered or comprehended by the majority. The larger the group, the worse this can be. In addition, some people will unhelpfully raise their hands to vote knowing little about the issue.

So here is the problem: How can a great number of people be reliably informed? How can they be made to discuss an issue until they have not only fully understood but also reached their own individual conclusion with regard to it? Without this a proper vote is just a bad joke.

It is possible to observe that a group discussion falls apart as soon as it comprises more than seven participants. The moment group size increases beyond seven, subgroups tend to form. Some will withdraw, fall asleep, or amuse themselves (e.g. playing with their mobile phones); others will begin to chat between themselves.

So monitoring the size of discussion groups appears to be the answer to our problem. A maximum of seven people will remain focused, will keep their interaction alive, will watch out for each other, will encourage comments and pick up each other's emotions. Seven means participation; more than seven means disinterest and disengagement.

More than seven results in the discussion and ongoing decision process being governed by the strongest and loudest only. The remainder cut themselves off. This is regrettable, as a lot of group intelligence becomes lost in this way. Many clever people simply are not strong and loud enough to make themselves heard. Sooner or later they give up.

The Speakers' Pyramid

The solution is simply to break a large group up into subgroups of five to seven, ask them to discuss the issue at hand, have them elect a speaker, and have that speaker report to the forum.

Assuming you had a group of thirty members you would break it up into six subgroups of five each. They would each determine their speaker. After this is done you would have five speakers sitting around a table to finalize the discussion and reach a decision.

Should an unforeseen controversy present itself, where the speakers do not feel entitled to represent without first consulting their group, a "second discussion wave" could be staged in the same way. All the speakers would return to their corresponding groups, discuss the novel turn in the issue to decision point, and return to the panel discussion.

Note that the speakers do not have to be the same persons as in the first "wave". If a subgroup (let us call them a "cell") considers that for the second wave a different speaker should be chosen, they would be entitled to do so. Speakers in this Speakers' Pyramid are not posts or offices entrusted to their holders for a fixed time period; they are simply functions (or hats). The moment that function is no longer needed, the office or post is redundant.

So far we have not dealt with a pyramid, only with a representation system on two levels. The pyramid idea will become more obvious the moment group size increases. Let's take the example of a small village of 2100 inhabitants. There is a plan to replace the small old gym with a big new one, and since this issue has already raised some controversy between various parties the mayor wishes to consult the villagers directly. Three hundred cells of seven each are formed, simply by neighbours meeting each other. This is the base level of the pyramid, its ground floor. Let's call it BL for "base level".

Each of the 300 cells on the Base Level arrives – after thorough and heated discussions! – at a decision or at least at a well-founded representation of the relevant pros and cons. Three hundred speakers are chosen, one for each cell.

Those 300 speakers get together in new cells of five to seven each, forming 43 cells. We are now on the first floor of the pyramid, one level up from the base (base level plus one, or BL+1).

Each of the 43 cells has its conference. Each elects a speaker to take the decision process one level higher up to the second floor of the pyramid, BL+2. So we get 43 speakers on BL+2.

On BL+2 the 43 speakers form six cells of six members and one cell of seven, a total of seven cells. In each cell the issue "new gym or no new gym?" is discussed through to decision point.

Once again each of these seven cells elects its speaker. Thus the third floor of the pyramid is formed, BL+3. Being seven, they form one single cell only. They compare their views on the gym issue. From this last cell of seven, one single speaker is chosen.

This single speaker is the representative of all the villagers. We have now reached the fourth floor of the pyramid, BL+4.

The representative now goes to meet the mayor, and offers him a differentiated and balanced view of what the people of the village think of the building project in question. This meeting should happen in public.

This talk between "the representative of the people concerned" and "the leading authority" may, however, not lead to the final word on the matter. It is possible that a whole new view or context may emerge, and a new question would have to be formulated by the mayor, to be discussed by the people in a new discussion wave. Before an issue is fully settled, quite a number of discussion waves may be needed.

This may take time but has the obvious advantage that everybody who cares was permitted to be part of the process. It is possible that it would not really take very long. If you allow one week each for the Base Level and the three floors to form, and talk the matter through to a good result, it would take only four weeks total before the Group Representative could speak to the

Authority on the final fourth floor. This is not by any standard a long time for a democratic process.

For a large company of 20,000 employees it would require only six levels for the boss to reach the ground floor; for a nation of 80 million it would be ten levels. Not a lot, really.

Obviously large group discussions, comprising thousands of people who live far apart from each other, cannot possibly be staged through personal meetings on a neighbourhood level. For that it would take an internet solution and the corresponding software (the ramifications of which have been worked out – just write an e-mail to the author of this book).

Rules of the Speakers' Pyramid

When a group has more than seven members it should divide into subgroups numbering between three and seven. We call this a "cell". People are not ordered who to get together with in a cell. Preferably a cell should be formed on the basis of personal closeness as this is the best prerequisite for communication to flow openly and speedily.

Within a cell matters are discussed until clarified. Agreement need not be expected, but rather clarification of viewpoints.

Each cell elects a speaker. He is simply a person whom the cell trusts and respects to represent its views. The role of the speaker is the outward representation of the wishes, needs, intentions, and proposals of the cell. The election is conducted through open discussion. This vote must be unanimous.

A speaker is responsible for fully and completely conveying the message of his cell. He may not tarry in communicating it, lose it, change it, or withhold it.

If a cell does not feel adequately represented by its speaker, it has three possible courses of action: a) The cell corrects him and gives him a second opportunity. – b) The cell asks him to step down, and another speaker is elected. – c) The cell excludes him if his failing is correspondingly severe, or if the cell feels incapable of correcting him, and elects another.

After each cell has elected its speaker, all the speakers get together to discuss the issue at hand. This occurs one level above the base level BL, and is therefore on BL+1.

Should the number of speakers on BL+1 be higher than seven, they would (in accordance with Rule 1) in their turn form cells.

After the discussion within the cells of BL+1, each cell elects a speaker. They meet one level higher up, on BL+2. This "distillation process" continues upwards through as many levels as needed. It finds its natural end on a level BL+n when only one single speaker is left. He is the true representative of the group which has created him. We call him the "Pyramid President".

The Pyramid President conveys the message of his group to the outside authority which has initiated, or was the reason for, this process, be it a headmaster, an executive director, a mayor, or a board of directors. The Pyramid President discusses the matter with the Authority, and then communicates the result to the group, be it to all at once by a public announcement, or by communicating it personally to the speakers of the cell which elected him, and they in turn communicate it to their cells, until the result has "percolated down" to the original base level.

A new "discussion wave" might now ensue. Wave follows after wave, until the matter has been discussed to its end and an "optimum solution" is reached, i.e. a solution which has the most advantages, and does the least damage, to the parties concerned. With each wave the participating cells may consist of different group members; the speakers may also be different. Equally, the Pyramid President could be a different person each time.

The magic of manipulation

We have seen that people see the world through their emotions as if they were wearing sunglasses of different hues. Given this, they decide strongly on an emotional basis and not strictly factually. Much as they may try to judge strictly factually, they will still get affected by their emotions without being aware of this.

Since emotions are the filters through which one looks at one's environment, it follows that you can govern the perception of people by influencing their emotions. The means to do this is called "PR" – public relations.

The art of PR was originally developed by Edward L. Bernays, a nephew of Sigmund Freud. Bernays lived from 1891 until 1995, and so not only created something new but also saw it through to its full development. His clever use of PR changed the face of the world. Without Bernays the United Fruit Company would not have controlled the governments of Central America, nor would women as a symbol of freedom and independence have started to smoke, nor would modern wars be fought by hired PR agencies rather than the military.

The use of symbols made the difference between the old-fashioned style of advertising and the studied use of public relations in the style of Bernays. He used or created emotionally charged symbols. That was the secret behind his magic.

The magic of PR serves to control and direct the emotions of people, be it potential customers in the marketplace, or one's political opponents.

In order to achieve this effect, PR compares the new with the known. In this way the emotions of the known become attached to the new. And so the new concept appears as good, or as bad, as the known.

Example: the Rolls Royce car is a symbol of British aristocracy. Wishing to sell some cheap jewellery, you would photograph it lying on the bonnet of a Rolls Royce, and the onlooker will immediately feel, by association, that he is looking at some really significant pieces of jewellery.

**People see what they like to see. Or what they
have been trained to see.**

Through PR people are encouraged to see things, persons or situations in a good or a bad light, depending on where you want to drive them. You create an image for them to see and follow. People then do not see the thing, the person or the situation itself, but an image specifically created for them. They do not see what's in front of them; instead they see a picture in their mind.

Control by means of agreement

Skilful PR does not lie. It simply puts some more emphasis on certain points, and less on others. It portions the truth in handy bits which can be easily swallowed by the receiver.

By holding on to a truth you feel better, in that there is less doubt and uncertainty in your life. This is the purpose of PR. It provides a well-tailored truth which offers a feeling of security to the players.

What do you think is true? – Whatever you can agree with.

Thus PR controls the emotions of people by creating agreement.

Whether what is agreed with is really and factually true is an entirely different question. Interestingly, what is really real does not count; what matters for people is what they *think* is real.

Everybody, each for himself, habitually views things the way he wants to have them. Unknowingly each person creates his own world. Everybody sees the world as he deems it right. This is a mechanism of the human psyche.

Without this impulse towards participation and co-creation of the environment, PR would have no effect. For it is only because people create pretences for themselves, continuously, that can one pretend to them. It is a habit.

Reality is therefore not created by passively agreeing with something that's been offered to you to believe in; it is an active process. It is created through active participation: namely through your personal contribution to what's being offered.

"Oh, what he says must be true; he's a scientist." – "She's the queen; she wouldn't lie, would she?" – "We've always done it this way, so it must be right." – "All the papers say it, and it was on the telly too!"

The gullible person slides without any resistance into such agreements. A critical person will try to hold his own against them.

The moment you have a viewpoint of your own, you will not easily be persuaded. But here is the trouble: none of the gullible ones will believe you. You might end up a martyr and be burnt at the stake for a truth that is not shared.

Expansion

By means of PR one can steer players and counter-players. Regarding one's fellow players, one would strengthen their faith in the attainability of their ideals. Regarding counter-players, one would discourage them concerning their ideals.

This way, one can make one's own team feel victorious, and can create apathy within the opposing team.

What is the strongest motor for production? High morale and enthusiasm. What is the most effective brake? Disappointment, frustration. In both cases you are looking at emotions.

In the same way that PR can come to grips with low moods and sinking morale, PR can increase production within one's own team. Or it can, by skilful propaganda, make the high mood of the enemy crumble. It can attract people to things and into areas they previously did not consider.

PR is more than merely advertising one's products to the public. PR is more than sales talk.

PR serves expansion.

PR and sales success

Selling functions in accordance with the principles described above. The moment a customer sees a product, he is often in a state of doubt. Should he buy or should he not? This doubt constitutes an emotional sales barrier: the customer cannot make a decision.

A skilled salesman uses PR in order to guide the attention of his customer towards his yet unattained ideals. He has his customer look at the product in the light of these ideals. He guides the attention of his customer not only to the quality of his product but mainly to the consideration of how much this product will help the customer make his dreams come true.

First the skilled salesman finds out which ideal state the customer wants to achieve through the product in question. He gets his customer to describe this ideal state in glowing colours.

The salesperson will then begin the real act of the sales procedure. He will point out how much the product in question can actually contribute to the realisation of the ideal state envisioned by the customer. He may perhaps point out an item even more suitable to the customer's purposes, something the customer never thought of, something twice as costly and three times as pleasing as the item the customer originally came into the shop to buy.

When the sale is made, the customer will be highly satisfied. Or – and this is the other possibility – customer and salesman alike come to the conclusion that the product at hand does not serve for realising the ideal state of the customer, and so they happily part.

By assisting the customer to realise what he really wants, the salesman turns his customer's doubts into certainty. The customer is now sure that he wants to either buy or not.

The skilled salesman happily achieves a clear yes or a clear no. In either case the salesman will be recommended by his customer as honest and reliable. Both have won.

By having kept his communication line with the customer clean, the salesman knows that this customer will one day return.

PR serves expansion.

5

Ethics

Our game has started running now; it is ticking over well. We have worked out a concept, we have organised, communicated, motivated, and now are producing. So it is running – but not always the way it should. It does have its ups and downs. Sometimes things go right; sometimes they go wrong.

Right and wrong

"Right" and wrong" is the subject matter of ethics. We will discuss the philosophy of this in the next section of this chapter. In the present section we are going to look at right and wrong from a merely practical viewpoint.

By "right" we mean that the game is moving in the direction of the ideal state we have envisioned for it. "Wrong" means it is deviating from that line.

In terms of statistics you would talk about upward and downward trends indicating whether it is going the right way or the wrong way, depending on your criteria.

When the dynamics of ups and downs become out of control, action needs to be taken. We should do a situation analysis. It serves to stabilise upward trends and to curb downward trends.

The Situation Analysis

First step: Prepare an account, or chronicle of the situation. A chronicle is a written record of events in the sequence in which they happened. A chronicle, if it is well worked out, will show you by date and even time of day:

Which decisions were made and by whom? Which particles, including money, entered and left the playing field and who was responsible? Who entered the game as a player or customer, and who left it?

You are looking for decisions, actions and statistics caused by fellow players or counter-players. What caused the initial downward trend? What subsequently occurred, when, where and how? Who was there? Time, place, circumstances, sequence of events, persons involved – who had which responsibility?

In collecting this information, even small, seemingly unimportant events should be noted, because they might be of unexpected importance in the analysis which is to follow as the next step.

Second step: Find the *apparent* beginning. The apparent beginning is the point in time when the uptrend or downtrend became obvious. The chronicle will clearly show when the trend started to change and what conditions prevailed at the time.

Third step: Find the *actual* beginning. Now follow up all relevant and pertinent indicators which appeared days and weeks before the apparent beginning, and may have contributed to the change of the trend. Search for the earliest indicators of the change of the trend. This way you work your way towards the *actual* beginning.

It never started when you noticed it. It started earlier. Always!

Fourth step: Make a list of plus points and minus points. A plus point is any event which falls in line with the attainment of the ideal state envisioned for the game. A minus point is any indication of a deviation or departure from the ideal state. Plus points and minus points are facts, not opinions. They refer to observable and recorded decisions, actions and statistics leading off the ideal state.

Facts can be proven. There is evidence for them. Opinions are deductions based on facts.

An opinion that is not based on facts has no validity.

In summary: assign plus and minus points to the facts observed, i.e. to statements, actions, and any seemingly pertinent phenomena, that were observed by known witnesses. Do not use any data based on imagination or hearsay.

Fifth step: Find the real reason. How could it have happened in the first place? The real reason for one's trouble is never God in heaven, the weather, the stars, or a butterfly beating its wings at the other end of the world. Even if it were so, it is not something about which we could do anything. But what we can do something about are our decisions and our organisation. One should therefore assume that when things go wrong it could be due to bad organisation and wrong decisions: concrete decisions, made by concrete people at a concrete moment.

The real reason, if worked on, will change the trend towards the better. This positive change proves that you have indeed found the real reason. When the situation does not take a positive turn, the real reason was not found.

Therefore do your analysis, find the real reason for the situation, and start immediate action in order to stabilise the uptrend or curb the downtrend.

When you have found the real reason, the situation will revert to the better.

Sixth step: Start corrective actions. You will have to adjust the game to the current conditions and put it on a new basis so as to avoid a recurrence of the detrimental situation.

This means: immediate handling of the danger points. Immediate correction or dismissal of the people involved. And then: new policies, adjustment of rules. Thus new channels for the game, and the attainment of its ideal state, are provided.

Ethics and morals

By dictionary definition the words "ethics" and "morals" are very similar. You'll find "ethics" defined in terms of "morals" and vice versa, as if the two terms were interchangeable.

"Ethics" comes from Greek, "morals" from Latin. Both mean "customs, cultural habits".

However, these terms are not generally used interchangeably. By implication there is a difference between ethics and morals. Perhaps this difference goes back to the original meaning of these two words: although they both mean "customs", ethics has the further meaning of "character, nature".

Someone with character emphasises his special features, his personal profile. He highlights the difference between himself and others. He sticks to his principles. Quite often he has worked towards his principles arduously throughout his life.

When you are ethical, you are true to yourself. You recognise the difference between right and wrong, and act accordingly. You make your own decisions on matters of behaviour and performance.

A moral person follows the crowd. He draws his convictions from the great reservoir provided by the traditions of his culture. He has no need to think for himself.

This does not by any means imply that ethical people are wise and good, and moral people stupid and bad. Nothing to do with it! Those living by their personal convictions, regardless of how well considered, do not always create good effects on the life of others. And those who take care to act in accordance with traditional morals, even if obediently and without too much reflection, do not always create bad effects.

There are plenty of aspects which would need clarification; a practical definition could be defined as follows:

Ethical is the attempt to act in the correct way in view of the context of the situation at hand, as much as one can see of this context, and considering as many recognisable factors as possible. Personal responsibility plays a senior role.

Moral is the attempt to do it right on the basis of customs, tradition and etiquette. Personal responsibility plays a minor role.

Both ethics and morals follow the same purpose: to facilitate an easier life and better survival. They constitute the attempt to put order into the chaos of life.

The principal difference being: someone acting morally can easily refer to decisions previously made by a majority. He takes these majority decisions as his guideline. However, acting ethically, a person's own individual decisions are made. He follows his own inner knowledge, accepting full responsibility in each new situation.

Ethics is very much a matter of "the situation as it appears *now*". Traditions, customs, rules and regulations *are* a component part of that situation! They would certainly be considered. Ignoring morals would lead to "bad ethics".

Ethics is morals critically analysed.

Individual ethics depend on the power of judgement and the experience of a player; in a word, on his competence: on his knowledge, his ability to control, and his willingness to accept responsibility for the consequences of his decisions.

Ethics is highly personal. It is a matter of honour and integrity. It is not enforceable. Morals, however, are usually established through a moral code. In many cases such a code even exists in writing. Consequently morals can be enforced: "Stop it! One does not do that!"

Who is "one"? And what could "one" object to about what I happen to be doing? How does stopping me make sense with reference to the situation at hand right this moment? What ideal state in the mind of the person stopping me would justify this stop?

Ethics would consider this; morals would not. That is the difference between morals and ethics.

Morals are instilled within culture. They are expressed in the laws of church and state. Not everybody is in agreement and there are always individuals and groups who seek their own solutions. They attempt to put order into their lives according to their own wisdom. By doing so they might go against the general agreement of the culture. Thus they are considered immoral although they may not actually harm anyone.

An individual person will consider his solutions ethical when his survival chances are increased thereby. The representatives of the culture, however, will not always consider bright ideas of individual people acceptable. Particularly when they see hallowed customs and traditions endangered – or the privileges of powerful lobby groups threatened.

Considerable friction can build up between general morals and individual ethics when two sets of survival solutions work against each other.

Three levels of ethics

The ethics level a person operates upon is dependent on his ability to review a situation and see it in its context. It is dependent on how far a player is able to look over the fence around his own garden patch. The bigger the picture viewed, the higher the ethics level – given that there is also empathy and compassion. An emotionally hard person will always act and decide in an inhuman way, regardless of how well he is capable of viewing the situation.

Lowest level: egotistical ethics

Egotistical ethics is strictly one-sided: "As long as there's something in it for me, that's what counts." Egotistical ethics is used not only by single individuals but also by a family, a group or a whole nation. All falls under the headline of "we are best".

Egotistical ethics can be defined as taking without giving; exploiting without restoring; depleting without nourishing. No exchange is offered.

Such solutions appear seemingly fast and effective, and therefore might impress one as rational, efficient and highly economical – but only initially. In their wake follow many difficulties because a lot of porcelain is broken. In the long run egotistical solutions turn out not to be rational but actually insane.

The standard: mutual ethics

This is two-sided. You fundamentally look after yourself but are willing to temporarily take another on board as long as he appears to further your purposes. In reality it is a partnership based on mutual egotism: "You and I are getting together on this deal and both of us are going to get something out of it. You and I are going to be straight with each other. The rest of the world is none of our concern."

This is the ethics of many business people and politicians. You join together, two or three against the rest of the world. Today like this, tomorrow like that. As the advantages change, variation in allegiances follow. The benefits of the moment conceal potential long-term difficulties. There is no loyalty. This again lacks sanity.

The top: compassionate ethics

This is defined as an all-encompassing view. It considers the welfare of all and everything. It desires the best for everybody. The widest possible context is taken into consideration. Preferably all participants should get something out of the solution found. At least as many as possible should get as much as possible. This is what we call the optimum solution. *Optimum* means: the best one can do under the circumstances.

Compassionate ethics strives for optimum solutions.

Optimum solutions are not always comfortable. Nor are they always popular. Frequently the majority would prefer not vote for them, because the majority seeks quick and easy solutions. Change is often seen as arduous and burdensome, and compassionate ethics often implies much change, particularly when moving up from lower ethics levels. Therefore the troubles, efforts and cost which accompany that change tend to be overstated. Only later, after their life quality has risen, will the majority be happy, and perhaps even be grateful.

Optimum solutions are not optimum because the majority votes for them, but because they can be proven to enhance a situation. This can be measured through products and statistics.

Optimum solutions cannot be enforced. It takes considerable PR in the true (!) definition of the word to sell them to people. However, once the solution presented is recognised to be in accordance with the ideals of the group, people will conform despite all their initial complaints about potential difficulties.

A further characteristic of optimum solutions is that they are "traceless". They do not leave a negative imprint; they do not leave a dirt trail which continues into the future. They do not bear within themselves the germ for future catastrophes. They are far-sighted.

With short-sighted decisions the solution of today creates the problems of tomorrow. Not so with optimum solutions.

Integrity

Good and reliable production can be maintained only by players with integrity. Integrity signifies a state of being whole, untouched and unaffected: being of one piece with no cracks. It means the absence of inner conflicts and contradictions, and of the consequential friction.

A person content within himself, whose being, doing and having are in tune with each other, has integrity. He does not seek unusual compromises. He remains true to himself. Being and remaining whole he is, in a way, "holy".

The life concept of a person can be seen best in terms of the ideals he is striving to attain. What desired reality is he attempting to realise? This shows unmistakeably which way that person is heading.

In an optimum game its Game Concept is supported by each player with his individual personal life concept. Such a game would have unshakeable integrity.

Conversely the integrity of a game is strained to the extent that the personal convictions of individual players deviate from the Game Concept. This is demonstrated through emotional tensions and bad temper.

A scale of integrity

No-one is found to be continually in a state of 100% integrity or 100% non-integrity. There is no "black or white" but many shades of grey with various states phasing into each other.

In order to reach a judgement on integrity, you will have to determine how far the existing situation deviates from the ideal state to which it relates. The ideal state is the yardstick. Without it the ethical value of a situation, i.e. its integrity, cannot be judged.

The existing situation is how it is. The ideal state is the way it should be. The further the two come apart, the lower the integrity level of the game, or any of its players. Conversely, the smaller the deviation, the higher the integrity level.

In the event that a given situation fully matches the ideal state, the highest possible integrity level for that game or player has been achieved.

From an external viewpoint that particular game may still be viewed very critically. For integrity, i.e. the lack of deviation from an ideal state, reflects only the inside viewpoint. However, a game operating on a one-sided or two-sided ethics level, rather than on an all-encompassing one, could still have integrity.

As an example, a war is never loved by anyone except by those who start it. Most wars are motivated by egotistical ethics. Nevertheless, the government and the military planning a war consider it and its aims in keeping with the highest principles of the nation. Doubtless there is integrity – even if on a low ethics level.

The integrity levels described in the next section refer to the attitude a player has to the game in which he is participating. They refer to his *being*.

Integrity levels do not appear in the form of products and statistics – not in the *doing*. They can be recognised through statements betraying the inner convictions of a player. Such statements will reflect whether there is a gap or not between the personal life concept of the player and the management concept of the game in which he participates.

A player without any such conflict is in the highest possible integrity condition. He is fully integrated in the game and in the group. His game and his life are in tune with each other. His being is in order, thus he is whole. (His doing and having will suffer the usual ups and downs and can be measured in terms of production levels, as covered in the next section of this chapter.)

Integrity levels dovetailed with production levels
A highly disciplined player who is not convinced of the game in which he is participating (being), may nevertheless be a very high achiever (doing and having). Much as his integrity condition is low, his production condition may still be high. This is reflective of his discipline and willpower.

Eventually, however, low integrity levels will lead to low

production levels. This is because a player who is not particularly interested in the game, is doubtful about it, or openly opposes it, will not have the energy to maintain production for an extended period of time. He may be highly competent professionally, but when he no longer feels emotionally close to the game, his production will go down at some stage.

The reverse is also true: a player can produce rather badly despite his full conviction of the value of the game. Despite full integrity he has meagre results. Why is that? Perhaps he is lacking experience. He may need additional training. Perhaps he is simply not suited to the post. A matter of competence, nothing further, which can be easily corrected.

Integrity levels

The integrity levels, beginning with the lowest, are as follows: confusion – irresponsibility – identity conflict – doubt – integration – full integrity. Confusion would constitute the deepest deviation from the ideal state of flawless integrity.

Each player can be placed on one or another of these levels, depending on the extent of his "integrity gap". With each level there is a "Remedy" on how to move up out of that level.

How can you recognise the correct level? The best proof is when the application of its Remedy brings a change for the better.

So first have a good in-depth talk with the player in question and find out where the trouble lies. Go through the Remedies with him to see which one might apply. Eventually he will have a realisation, and brighten up. Then have him move up level by level, Remedy after Remedy.

It is quite difficult for a player to see his own integrity level and apply its Remedy by himself. Usually it takes a trusted person to share an enlightening talk, and reach a realisation.

Confusion

Indicators: The player does not know which game he is in. He lives in a different world. He is not in touch. Perhaps he is lost because it is all new and overwhelming. In people under the influence of shock, drugs or alcohol, this is easily observed.

Someone in confusion is not a player in the real sense of the word. He does not know the concept of the game of which he is part, and possibly not even his own life concept. He is totally upside down.

Remedy: Find a stable orientation point within the game: another player, a rule, a product, a location, or some other aspect of the game. Something which can be used to hold on to, and be used as an anchor. Should you be very badly confused (as for example under alcohol, drugs or shock), look for a quiet corner where you can come to your senses. Knock against a wall with your flat hands. Grab tables and chairs with your hands and feel them. Ascertain to yourself that walls, chairs and tables exist for real. Use them as orientation points until you feel stabilised.

Then get your bearings on the surroundings and the ongoing game.

Result: You have found out where you are located in the game, and which game is being played here. You are now one integrity level further up. Apply the Remedy for irresponsibility.

Irresponsibility

Indicators: The player is not sure about the consequences of his actions. He does not know his hat or was not told how to wear it properly. He inadvertently makes mistakes and creates chaos without realising what he is doing. He appears thoughtless, clumsy, sloppy or careless. He makes irritating and disturbing statements. He does not quite pull his weight. He may have some idea about the game, but has no idea that people actually notice him, let alone rely on him. Even if he outwardly appears to know the concept of the game, and to agree with it, it may turn out on closer questioning that he does not quite relate to it as one would expect. Therefore one cannot rely on him.

Remedy: Find out that you exist as a player and that your actions have consequences on others and on the game.

Result: Once you have recognised what effects you are causing, you are in the next condition up. Apply the Remedy for identity conflict.

Identity conflict

Indicators: The player more or less understands the concept of the game in which he is participating. However, he certainly does not know his position in the game. Where does he really belong? He may understand the description of his post, but what he is actually doing might be something entirely different from what is expected. What his hat sounds like on paper, and what he really does, seems contradictory. So what role does he actually play? Who or what is he really being?

There is a gap between expectation and reality. The player suffers from a conflict between expected identity and actual identity.

Remedy: Look at what you are supposed to be being, doing, and having in this game, and what you are actually being, doing, and having. Make yourself fully aware of all aspects. Drop all pretences and false promises and glorious labels; see them for what they are. Face the truth, painful as it may be.

Result: You know now who you are – but do you really wish to be that? Asking yourself that question puts you one level up. Apply the Remedy for doubt.

Doubt

Indicators: The player sits between two chairs, and does not quite know where he belongs. He knows the concept of the game he is in, he has experienced it being played, he fully understands his own position in it, but he is not sure if he can back it up fully and wholeheartedly.

Remedy: Work out, in writing, the concept of the game you are in, in particular of the hat you are wearing. Then work out a Game Concept for your whole life, a life concept.

Now that you can see the gap between the two concepts, you can determine if they are compatible or not, and whether you wish to go or to remain.

Make your choice known to those it actually concerns. For the team that you have decided against, you are now a non-player. Merely that. You have not turned into an enemy, at least not necessarily so. In principle this has nothing to do with aggressiveness or animosity. For it is possible to decide without animosity that one is of a different opinion with regard to a particular activity, goal, or game.

Result: Should you have chosen to remain with your team or game, you are now on the next level up. Apply the Remedy for integration as required. This is dependent on the extent that your doubtful attitude has put the game at risk or endangered team mates.

Integration

Indicators: The player has been doubtful of the game, and perhaps has made some scathing remarks regarding the game, some players, and his role in it. He disturbed the peace; he did not contribute to a pleasant team spirit. He may also have caused some actual damage, either materially, or by upsetting other players, or both. Although he has now changed, the group still wonders if they can trust him; ill feelings remain.

Remedy: Make it known to your team mates that you feel part of the team. Demonstrate through your actions and behaviour that you fully support the shared Game Concept, and your role within.

Apologize. Buy flowers and chocolates. Make up for the damage you have done and the confusion you have caused. Restore the trust of your team mates in you. Make up for any material damage.

If appropriate, obtain official acknowledgement from your team mates that they really want you back in the game. If your amends were sufficient and convincing, you will not find anyone giving you a hard time here.

Result: Being back with the group brings you to the next integrity level up: working towards full integrity.

Full integrity

Indicators: The player knows and understands the Game Concept, and backs it up with his life concept. He appreciates the team, and is appreciated in return.

Remedy: This is not so much a remedy but some good advice on how to remain at this level. It is simple yet hard: Remain aware at all times. Look out for any disparaging indicators. Do not let others fool you, and do not fool yourself. Do not compromise your loyalty in any way.

Production levels

Integrity breakdowns cause a lowering of one's production. Production also can be viewed in terms of levels. They are, from the lowest one upwards: non-existence – danger – emergency – normal operation – prosperity – abundance.

Non-existence

Indicators: You have worked out your Game Concept to begin a new game, or have been given a hat within an ongoing game, but as yet nobody is aware of your function. Even though you may know some people on a personal basis you have not made yourself a name yet as "the new player".

Group communications and interactions run the way they did before you arrived. They run around you as if you were not there.

Should you as a self-employed person have started a business, you will soon become painfully aware of the fact that the market does not know you.

Remedy: Build up contacts. Make yourself known. Find out what is needed and wanted and what of that you could produce. Produce it.

Result: You have managed to draw some attention towards yourself; you have delivered services and products. This is a good start, but you may still run into danger. Apply the Remedy for danger.

Danger

Indicators: As you are still new in the game you can easily make mistakes. You may even encounter hostility from competing players or teams. There are rules and regulations, habits and customs you had not envisioned. You are at risk of getting pushed out of the game and sinking back into non-existence.

Remedy: Recognise the danger for what it is and handle it immediately. Firstly, before doing anything else, "extinguish the fire". Ignore all formalities, etiquette and time-honoured routines. You may have to act alone and bypass individual players to save the whole.

Prepare a situation analysis. Filter out the real reason for this situation and formulate rules so that the danger may never occur again. Re-define and adjust the operational basis of your game. Formulate new rules as needed. Re-organise your own game.

Correct and discipline those concerned. This applies not only to perpetrators but also to victims. And to yourself, too! There are always many sides to any situation. Perhaps not only the actual perpetrators but also the victims acted inattentively and irresponsibly. They should all be heard. You are aiming at raising responsibility on all sides; you are not out for punishment and revenge.

Result: The danger has been handled. Increased activity to make up for production loss will be required, and will now have a positive result. But you are not through it all yet. There will be the occasional difficulty, the unexpected emergency. Apply the Remedy for emergency.

Emergency

Indicators: Production statistics fluctuate. In terms of sales, personnel, production the occasional difficult situation occurs. Yet if recognised it can all be handled simply by doing some extra work.

Remedy: Advertise, promote, work hard, produce. Keep your discipline tight. Be watchful.

Result: When you have managed to stabilise things you can relax. You are approaching normal operation.

The difference between danger and emergency

An emergency can be handled by being clever, thrifty, and doing plenty of hard work. These same actions will not help in a danger situation, however.

Danger means: something unexpected is wrong, something as

yet unseen. In an emergency it is all very obvious, but in a danger situation there is a hidden source of trouble. Danger means you are heading for disaster yet have no idea what is wrong. You may not even be aware *that* something is wrong.

An emergency has an obvious appearance; danger does not. It follows that the most important feature of danger is: production or sales go down and do not go up *despite* intensive work. No matter how hard you may try, there is little change. So there must be a different reason for the situation other than a mere lack of eagerness and zeal.

Example: When you are rowing your boat across a lake on a stormy and rainy day, water will collect in the boat, which of course you bail out. There is also the occasional bit of spray, but that's alright – some more bailing handles it nicely. You are in a slight emergency without any worries. Some hard work will fix it. Until you discover that the water level inside the boat is rising, and keeps on rising, despite all the bailing out you are doing! There must be a hole in the boat. All the bailing you might do will not keep the water from rising. So you need to find the hole and plug it. Only after that will bailing water out pay off again. Before this it was a fruitless effort.

Danger means: something other than meets the eye is wrong.

Normal operation

Indicators: Despite the ups and downs there is a general upward trend. No crashes.

Remedy: Do not change anything in a big way. All is running well, so leave it alone. Keep an eye on it; nurse it on. Each time there is a downward trend do a situation analysis. Find out what caused the change. Recognise negative trends and catch them before they can stall your upward development. Watch for further positive trends.

Result: Things start moving faster. Your statistics settle in on a higher range. You are nearing the level of prosperity.

Prosperity

Indicators: You are suddenly in demand. Orders come in from all sides, clogging your mailbox. There is a definite flow towards you. Statistics have moved up into an unprecedented high range and have levelled out there. You feel confident in the application of your knowledge and your skills. You have more money, more means and more possibilities than ever before. But do not fool yourself! The big mistake you could make here is to believe that you have reached full success.

So do not be careless and indulge in luxury. Be very diligent about how you spend your time and money so as to stabilise this pleasant state.

Remedy: Do not waste time and money. Pay all bills in sight. Take all incomplete actions to their good end. Go for independence in all respects. Invest all your time and money in training more staff and creating better means of production. You are pretty close to the realisation of the ideal state which you envisioned for the game and for yourself!

Result: You are getting close to a state of abundance.

Abundance

Indicators: The existing situation is close to the ideal state you have been striving to attain, even matching it occasionally. The statistics have settled in a very high range. You are in a position of power and influence. You have made a name for yourself and are firmly established in the market. You are now in the lucky position of having more money than you need. It is "playing money", meaning money with which you can freely experiment and explore new game possibilities, knowing that it will not hurt you if an experiment goes wrong.

The word "power", derived from the French word *pouvoir*, does not only mean that you are in the possession of money and political influence. It also means *you can do something perfectly* without limits. It means that you have an outstanding competence in your field, be it as an artist, a scientist or a businessman. It is all at your fingertips. Abundance!

Remedy: Keep up your old contacts and communication lines. Do not disconnect or become complacent. Do not interfere too much. Keep the trend stable. It is like normal operation except on a much higher level. Take care to delegate your hats and tasks to trustworthy players. Free yourself up for new and different games.

Result: Enjoy the game! And look out for the next one.

Passing your game on

Indicators: Being masterful and powerful, having achieved it all, you may now find your game considerably less challenging than before. A lessening of interest follows, which can be dangerous. Boredom leads to annoyance and annoyance to withdrawal.

One may feel inclined to withdraw from the communication lines one has built up over the years. One may ignore the vital contacts upon which alone one's condition of abundance and influence is resting. One's integrity may soften up. One may become inattentive, perhaps light-headed.

Out of light-headedness one makes mistakes. And suddenly the game breaks down. Overnight one may wind up in a condition of danger. From masterful performance down to danger – it can happen as fast as lightning.

It would have been a lot better if, at the right moment, you had passed your game on to others. Before initiating your own downfall you should have turned your game over to a successor, to rise to even greater heights yourself.

Yet there are also other reasons for turning a game over, and that is the usual way things go. For example you may have been given a different hat by order from above, or you must leave the game for some urgent reason. In contrast to the above this means that you have to delegate your hat in a non-optimum condition.

In either case, whether leaving voluntarily as a master or as "forced by fate", use the following Remedy.

Remedy (for the person leaving his post or game): Write up your hat; write up the complete Game Concept from the viewpoint of your hat. Point out in particular your successful actions so that your successor can go by them. Hand all information and all tools over to your successor. Tell him each and everything you have the faintest inkling of. Initiate him into all the secrets. If you do not do that, you will always keep one foot in your former game. You will not fully disconnect. You will never feel at rest.

Result: You have fully withdrawn from your former game. No further consultations need to be given. Let *them* do it. Do not look back.

Remedy (for the person taking over): Do not change anything. Do not turn everything upside down in order to show off as the new boss. Study the hat of your predecessor, in particular his successful actions. Observe the game and your position within it. Find out who is who. Be personal with people. Get to know them. Realise what integrity and production levels your various co-players (and yourself) are operating on, and handle accordingly.

Result: You have analysed the game in terms of integrity and production levels, and have firmly settled in. So good luck for attaining a level of abundance for yourself and the whole game!

Management by ethics

A player in a low condition of integrity represents a liability for other players. His lack of integrity leads to insufficient production. Others have to work for him. They have to wear his hat for him.

Frequently such a player will spread out his personal problems in front of other players. He will tell them about his difficulties with the game and with psychosomatic illnesses connected with that. He offloads his life upsets on his fellow players, spreads rumours, or keeps people from doing their job by being trivial.

Such a player does not give a good example. His presence demoralises. He pulls energy off the other players. They become tired and listless. Additional work appears from unknown sources, and it is definitely unnecessary work ("fake work").

There's only one remedy for this: to recognise the integrity level of the player, have a heart-to-heart talk with him, and ask him to apply the pertinent Remedy.

When you as a manager fail to do this, you will wind up on exactly the integrity and production level which you have omitted to assign to your fellow players. It works as sure as natural law.

Do not be lenient, and do not hesitate, as that might be your own downfall. But do not shoot with cannons where guns are sufficient.

Integrity and production levels help make one see what is wrong with the game. They must never be misused for putting pressure on fellow players. When you are rehabilitating fellow players whose ethics have collapsed, they can only be managed with tactfulness, friendliness and a light touch, not with rudeness or disdain. Humility paves the way.

Also the extent of the transgression of a player must be taken into consideration. Although a small doubt is in principle the same as a huge doubt, the application of the pertinent Remedy must be in proper proportion. Do not shoot at sparrows with artillery.

If an integrity or production level has been assigned correctly, you can see a smile of recognition on the face of the player, or perhaps a sigh of relief. And things will improve the moment the appropriate Remedy is put in action.

Integrity levels one can also apply to oneself. For one has a relationship not only with the game, one's hat and one's fellow players, but also with one's own life concept.

You could, for example, be in doubt about yourself or about your abilities. You could feel an enemy to yourself. You could be so confused that you no longer know where you stand regarding yourself. So you would be unhappy, naturally.

This of course would overshadow your general behaviour and your performance at work. In a state of low integrity you would not be able to fully wear your hat as a human being.

Good leadership would take such a personal matter in another into consideration. So quietly sit down with your fellow player and help him through the remedies step by step.

Two rights for all game players

At the highest level of ethics and motivation in a game all players would be fully self-determined. No duress would be used, no trickery, no secrecy. Everybody would feel and act duty-bound, in full awareness of the Game Concept and the present state of the game.

Naturally a team is kept together by co-ordination, consideration, and rules. People cannot just act alone. The core to a successful team is to have agreed on those rules self-determinedly and wholeheartedly.

Self-determinism, this highest ethical yardstick, is almost impossible to put into practice. Yet it should at least be mentioned, if only as a principle.

Self-determinism means you are granting each player the unshakeable right to enter a game on his own volition, and are permitting him to leave it on the same terms.

In an ethical game a player would be granted the right to enter as well as leave the game on his own determinism.

In reality, entering a game is usually a lot less complicated than getting out.

The trouble in getting out

Getting out elegantly and honourably is quite difficult. Why? Because of the agreements and relationships with other players one has developed, and because of the obligations one has accepted regarding one's hat.

Yet, much as one should not keep a player by force in a game he wishes to leave, one must make it also very clear to the person leaving that his departure will not go unnoticed.

Leaving a game has its consequences. There are two decisive factors determining the quality of a departure: What is the integrity level of the player leaving? What is the production level of his post?

A person who leaves hastily and leaves his post in a mess is not departing honourably. A person who spreads bad news about the game or team, before or after leaving, equally does not depart honourably.

A person not leaving honourably will later invariably indulge in justifications. A person indulging in justifications is hiding something. You can bet that he has left some dirt somewhere. It is his bad conscience that is making the noises.

A person leaving a team dishonourably, be it secretly or with a bang, in order to join another game or team, does not only leave broken china in his old team, but also constitutes a risk for his new team.

This is because the player who left his earlier team in the middle of some upset, and is therefore emotionally, financially, and perhaps even legally stressed, did not actually fully depart. He drags his low-integrity condition from one team to the next. For this reason he has not fully arrived in his new team.

With all the self-determinism in the world, a player departing in a low condition has neither left the old team properly nor arrived in the new team properly. He stands somewhere in between.

In order not to put themselves at risk, the players of the new team should ideally be entitled to demand that the new player cleans up his relationship with the old team and makes up for any damage he has done there. So that he may finally leave without any bad feelings on either side, and be received in the new team with good feelings on both sides. For only when he is on good terms with his old team can one welcome him whole-heartedly in the new team.

Is this asking for too much? It is. Can this be put in practice realistically? Probably not. But when you consequently think the whole thing through to its end, you do find the occasional very high yardstick, and that is always uncomfortable. But let us do it here, let us dream of a beautiful and happy organisation, let us dream this dream through to its end. And let us work on making it happen.

The value of games

Players in a team tend to take their game very seriously. They do not look beyond the fence and introvert into their game, its values, purposes, ideals, rules, goals, products, friends, and enemies.

They tend to evaluate their game from a viewpoint of one-sided ethics. As long as it is fun, everything is alright, they say. They are often quite naively and innocently egotistical.

A highly productive game, seen from the viewpoint of the participating players, will be highly valued since it furthers their survival and therefore is without question deemed ethical. Yet the same game, looked at from the viewpoint of other games and teams, may appear entirely unethical.

Example: A hunting party celebrates the successful end of the day. They have killed lots of does, rabbits, and pheasants, and had a great time. In contrast, nature protectionists and vegetarians will consider the event irresponsible, cruel, and condemnable.

So we can see that not only is each single player of a game individually operating on some level of ethics, production, and integrity, but also the game as such is on some level or other.

How the state of a game is judged, what value is attributed to it, depends entirely on the beholder. It depends on the context the beholder sees a game to be occurring in.

To evaluate a game correctly, one must look at its products, and how they affect other games, their players and the environment.

Only in terms of compassionate ethics can a game be correctly evaluated.

**BUSINESS
BOOKS**

Business Books encapsulates the freshest thinkers and the most successful practitioners in the areas of marketing, management, economics, finance and accounting, sustainable and ethical business, heart business, people management, leadership, motivation, biographies, business recovery and development and personal/executive development.